Puzzles
for Cat
Lovers

A fun, super variety of puzzles best enjoyed in the company of your favorite cat

Inspired by Faith

Puzzles For Cat Lovers
ISBN 978-1-7336250-5-0
Published by Product Concept Mfg., Inc.
2175 N. Academy Circle #201, Colorado Springs, CO 80909

©2019 Product Concept Mfg., Inc. All rights reserved.

Written and Compiled by Patricia Mitchell
in association with Product Concept Mfg., Inc.

Sayings not having a credit listed are contributed by writers
for Product Concept Mfg., Inc. or in a rare case,
the author is unknown.

Puzzles
for Cat
Lovers

*A kitten is in the animal world what
a rosebud is in the garden.*

Robert Southey

Here's a collection of puzzles all about cats – all kinds of cats! And throughout this book, you'll find all kinds of puzzles too! From crosswords to word searches, riddles to brainteasers, each puzzle is especially created for the cat-lover in you. So grab a pencil, curl up someplace comfortable, and start wherever you please – just like a cat!

Winding Way

Cats aren't known for taking the most direct route - unless it's to the food bowl, of course. In this puzzle, the last letter of the first answer to the first clue becomes the first letter of the second answer, and so on. The number of spaces indicates the number of letters in the answer.

1. Cats do this most of the day

1. __ __ __ __ __

2. Like most kittens

2. __ __ __ __ __ __ __

3. Word for an affectionate cat

3. __ __ __ __ __ __

4. Expert to see for a cat's lion cut

4. __ __ __ __ __ __ __

5. What a nuzzling cat might want

5. __ __ __

6. Persian, for example

6. __ __ __ __ __

7. Most housecats

7. __ __ __ __ __ __ __ __

8. Cat's favorite mint

8. __ __ __ __ __ __

9. Possible name for a cat with a spotted coat

9. __ __ __ __ __ __ __

Purrsonality!

Every cat was born with a triple measure of star power! How many three-letter words can you form from the word PERSONALITY? Common words only; no capitals, no plurals. We found 55!

P E R S O N A L I T Y

_____ _____ _____
_____ _____ _____
_____ _____ _____
_____ _____ _____
_____ _____ _____
_____ _____ _____
_____ _____ _____
_____ _____ _____
_____ _____ _____
_____ _____ _____
_____ _____ _____
_____ _____ _____
_____ _____ _____
_____ _____ _____
_____ _____ _____
_____ _____ _____
_____ _____ _____
_____ _____ _____
_____

A kitten is the delight of a household. All day long, a comedy is played out by an incomparable actor. ~Jules Champfleury

Cat-Tac

Each answer in this puzzle contains the word CAT or, read backward, TAC!

ACROSS
2. "Shoo!"
4. Barcelona's region
7. Disperse randomly
10. Seattle neighbor
12. Model's platform
14. Island off the coast of California
16. Football term

DOWN
1. Strategy

3. Provide food, as for a reception
5. Chimney
6. Glue to
8. Booklet of merchandise
9. Scornful, as a remark
11. Go at
12. Writer Willa
13. Unstated yet understood
14. Range grazers
15. Former gold coin in Europe

Oh, No!

Unscramble these common cat-related words, and then unscramble the shaded letters to finish the caption below!

S I H S

__ __ __ __

G R E T I

__ __ __ __ __

P J M U

__ __ __ __

A N P

__ __ __

U T A I T E D T

__ __ __ __ __ __ __ __

S I F H

__ __ __ __

C T N E S

__ __ __ __ __

Yesterday, she ate a whole skein. I'm afraid she's going to have...

Caption: __ __ __ __ __ __ __ !

Feline Word Search

Short hair, long hair, sleek or fluffy – there are all kinds of kitties to fill your home with love!

ABYSSINIAN	MUNCHKIN
ANGORA	NEBELUNG
BENGAL	OCICAT
BIRMAN	PERSIAN
BOBTAIL	RAGAMUFFIN
BOMBAY	RAGDOLL
BURMESE	RUSSIAN BLUE
CORNISH REX	SCOTTISH FOLD
EXOTIC	SIAMESE
HIMALAYAN	SIBERIAN
KORAT	SNOWSHOE
MAINE COON	SPHYNX
MANX	TONKINESE

```
V  Y  C  C  X  E  R  H  S  I  N  R  O  C  X
K  J  G  D  K  Q  O  K  E  B  B  L  M  I  Y
O  R  U  N  G  N  R  X  L  N  A  M  R  I  B
R  A  N  L  W  Y  O  N  A  I  R  E  B  I  S
A  Z  W  A  R  T  U  N  L  S  M  X  U  X  X
T  M  X  O  I  L  Y  O  I  I  U  W  N  S  Q
L  A  M  C  V  N  F  D  L  K  A  Y  G  A  C
H  I  B  A  M  M  I  T  O  L  H  T  X  K  M
E  N  C  N  H  K  L  S  W  P  O  C  B  A  E
H  E  X  G  D  M  W  H  S  T  J  D  N  O  V
C  C  B  O  M  B  A  Y  V  Y  A  X  G  U  B
S  O  B  R  W  F  R  W  N  X  B  C  G  A  M
I  O  S  A  A  P  U  I  A  J  S  A  I  I  R
A  N  V  L  X  J  L  N  Y  I  U  J  A  C  J
M  E  D  Z  V  P  P  D  Q  I  I  S  Z  T  O
E  U  D  L  O  F  H  S  I  T  T  O  C  S  N
S  L  E  B  N  S  N  O  W  S  H  O  E  W  I
E  B  S  P  A  G  P  E  R  S  I  A  N  H  F
R  N  E  I  Y  N  N  C  W  F  O  E  K  N  F
G  A  N  Q  A  U  W  X  N  L  M  D  I  G  U
Q  I  I  P  L  L  I  B  U  R  M  E  S  E  M
Q  S  K  G  A  E  Y  M  C  M  I  Y  J  G  A
D  S  N  Y  M  B  E  N  K  N  Z  S  Q  A  G
N  U  O  D  I  E  S  L  A  G  N  E  B  U  A
U  R  T  Z  H  N  R  Y  T  M  Z  C  C  E  R
```

Letter Swap

Change one letter of the word that answers Clue 1 to form a word that answers Clue 2. The lines indicate the number of letters in the answer.

Example:

Clue 1: Cat box contents .... L I T T E R
Clue 2: Sour .... B I T T E R

Clue 1: Cat's coat.................... ___ ___ ___
Clue 2: In favor of .... ___ ___ ___

Clue 1: Some cat food .... ___ ___ ___ ___ ___ ___
Clue 2: Eat lightly .... ___ ___ ___ ___ ___ ___

Clue 1: Kitten descriptor .... ___ ___ ___ ___
Clue 2: Silent............................ ___ ___ ___ ___

Clue 1: Contented cat sound .. ___ ___ ___ ___
Clue 2: Knitter's term............. ___ ___ ___ ___

Clue 1: Many a striped cat...... __ __ __ __ __
Clue 2: Talkative...................... __ __ __ __ __

Clue 1: Cat's foot features....... __ __ __ __ __
Clue 2: Gives applause .... __ __ __ __ __

Clue 1: What kittens like to do __ __ __ __
Clue 2: Speak to God .... __ __ __ __

Clue 1: What a cat might pick up __ __ __ __ __
Clue 2: Landscape .... __ __ __ __ __

Clue 1: Some cat coat markings __ __ __ __ __ __
Clue 2: Lighters........................ __ __ __ __ __ __

Clue 1: Angry cat sound .... __ __ __ __
Clue 2: Wild roses have them .. __ __ __ __

Clue 1: Polydactyl number....... __ __ __
Clue 2: Rule out........................ __ __ __

Mew Math

A breeder had a Persian kitten ready for adoption. The price was $5,000. One interested buyer offered the breeder $5,000 cash now. Another interested buyer asked the breeder if he would be willing to take $2,000 cash now, and $260 each month for 12 months.

Which is the best offer monetarily?

Cat and Mouse

In this flower field of felines, several mice are hiding.

Find 11  that are subtly hidden within the scene.

Catty Crossword

This puzzle is best solved in the presence of your favorite feline!

ACROSS

1. This puzzle's shape
3. Moved swiftly
7. Has dined
11. Rent out
13. Speak to
16. Golf ball holder
17. High-__, as of an image
18. Mindless
19. Hive dweller
20. Downcast

DOWN

1. Personal vehicle
2. Heavy weight
4. Autumn bloomer

5. French article
6. Running
8. Pasta choice (2 words)
9. Neverending
10. Cave mammal
12. Sharp curve
14. Former name of Indonesia, Abbrev.
15. Observe
21. Going down the tail, what the black squares look like

Cat Culprit

Sam Sport, an orange-striped tom, was a thief – no doubt about it! He was observed many times trotting back home with a towel, garden glove, or ball cap gripped tightly in his mouth.

One morning, Sam's human found five items on his porch: a pair of sunglasses, a mitten, a towel, an unopened seed packet, and a sun visor. Each item belonged to one of the five other families on the block: Jones, Brown, Smith, Dorel, and Hansen. Using the clues below, figure out the likely owner of each item.

1. No one in either the Dorel family or the Jones family wore sunglasses or sun visors.
2. The Dorels and Smiths often drive to the mountains to ski.
3. Jean Smith frequently hangs some of her laundry on the patio to dry.
4. No one in the Brown or Hansen family enjoys gardening.
5. Nadia Hansen is noted for her decorative sun visors.

	Sunglasses	Mitten	Towel	Seed Packet	Sun Visor
Jones					
Brown					
Smith					
Dorel					
Hansen					

The World's Most Purrfect Word Search

Find the bolded words in this word search.

All kinds of cats make **purrfect** friends,
whatever **color**, shape, or **size**–
A **cuddly-nuzzly** ball of **fur**,
a **whiskered**, winsome, paw-some **prize**!

They're **quick** to make themselves at **home**
and **occupy** your **favorite** chair–
And if you'd like to **sit** there too,
the **feline** might **agree** to **share**.

While some are quite **persnickety**,
some other cats are more **laidback**–
But all will **thrive** when **served** with **love**,
(and few would spurn a **midnight** snack).

From **kitten-sweet** to **tomcat-tough**,
each cat is **mew-y**, mew-y **fine**–
But I can say without a **doubt**,
the **world's** most purrfect **cat** is **mine**!

```
V U V F E L I N E N K C I U Q
R Y Y P E R S N I K E T Y S I
T C E M O H N K S T J O V C V
G A G M X K X A H S T T P O T
C M G P E W J G N A D M G L K
J C V R C Q I B U D I L U O B
I E K Z E N I D E V Z X R R O
X T D D E C N B E T B U O D
X I I I O R P D T H R I V E W
G R M D L S H F G H I B O R L
P O K I T T E N S W E E T H L
B V C E N U Q P P J L A G A C
S A H O R U T Z J O C U I U U
K F C D D A P L P A O D D A S
C U V H E Q H K I T B D H V E
Q B V P V P R S T A L H J R U
B J Z E R G D A C Y B D F E I
Y V M L E T C K N T E U V Y Q
W L P L S M C U M R C O T K G
E T Y J O W Z E E F L J M M J
M C P T Q Z G K F Q I O R U F
H V U D L F S E P R K E Z I S
B G C Y F I T X N I R E N I F
S V C C H W Y I M I K U B W H
Q W O W A E Z E S N M U P K J
```

Catty Compounds

Can you determine what compound word (one word composed of two other words) from the definitions given?

Example: Feline + bite   =   _CATNIP_

1. Tabby + gilled one   =   _____

2. Paned opening + ledge   =   _____

3. Bloomer + sleeper   =   _____

4. Body part + preside over   =   _____

5. Sky sight + ray   =   _____

6. Problem + creator   =   _____

7. Mouser + snooze   =   _____

8. Mimick + feline   =   _____

9. Swimmer + big dish   =   _____

10. Happy pastime + object   =   _____

11. Performance + not fresh   =   _____

12. Sugary + blood pumper   =   _____

Silly Puppy?

One day, when Oscar Tomcat was sitting in his yard with his friends, the puppy next door came outside. "Hey, guys," Oscar said, "let me show how you how dumb this dog is!" The cats approached the picket fence, and the puppy happily bounded over to them. Oscar held one bone in his right paw and two bones in his left paw. "Right or left?" The puppy grabbed the one bone in Oscar's right paw and scampered away. "See?" Oscar said. "Every time he takes one bone instead of two!"

But his friends thought the puppy was pretty smart. Why?

Kitten Caboodle

When mama cat wasn't looking, her five kittens decided to explore the house. The sound of a ripping window screen, however, found Mama dashing to the living room. She found all five kittens and one torn screen. "Someone has tried to climb the screen!" she said, looking at each one. "Who did it?" Only one kitten is telling the truth. Which one?

Winky: "Callie did it."
Fluff: "I saw Callie halfway up the screen."
Tom: "It was Callie."
Callie: "Winky isn't telling the truth."
Tortie: "What Winky said is true."

When Life Gives You Lemons...

Unscramble each word, and then unscramble the shaded letters for a fitting caption to the clue below!

"He just bit into a lemon!"

R E R S T O

⬤ _ _ ⬤ _ _ _ _

T P U S R O

_ ⬤ _ _ ⬤ _

S O S M L B O

_ _ ⬤ _ ⬤ _ _

S I R O U T T

_ ⬤ _ _ ⬤ _

Caption: _ _ _ _ _ _ _ _ !

Syllabic Sphinx

To complete this quote on the next page, fill in the blanks with the syllables found in the box. Some syllables may be split between two words, be used twice or stand as one word on its own. The number of spaces indicates the number and placement of letters.

IS	THE	USE
WAR	OUR	IN
MET	UMP	BE
OF	AT	LAP
BE	LAP	ADO
USE	TIS	BUT
TOY	ON	DOE

IF ___ ___ ___G J ___ ___ ___S

IN ___ ___ ___ OUR ___ ___ ___,

I ___ ___ ___ ___ ___CA ___ ___ ___

HE ___ ___ F ___ ___ D ___ ___ YOU;

___ ___ ___IF A C___ ___ ___ ___ ___S

___ ___ ___ SA ___ ___ ___H ___ ___G,

IT IS ___ ___ CA ___ ___ ___

Y ___ ___ ___ ___ ___ ___ IS

___ ___ ___MER.

Alfred North Whitehead

Wild Cats

In each sentence, there's a wild cat word hiding. Watch out – it could be anywhere!

1. If it's oleo, pardon me, I'd prefer butter.

2. The kabob caterer served tasty food.

3. Watch that magnificent stallion run!

4. My sister, Nadja, guaranteed our reservations.

5. In Puerto Rico, we were served pumarosas, or rose apples.

6. Believe me, Rosco, Ugarit was an ancient port city.

7. She thought she'd gain prestige really quickly once people knew where she'd been.

Collections of Cats

A large group of people is called a crowd, but what are groups of cats called? In this puzzle, the vowels have been inserted, but it's up to you to fill in the rest!

1. Cats   __ __ O __ __ E __

2. Kittens   __ I __ __ __ E

3. Tigers   __ __ __ E A __

4. Lions   __ __ I __ E

5. Jaguars   __ __ A __ O

6. Leopards   __ E A __

7. Cheetahs   __ O A __ I __ I O __

Happy Cats

See if you can find all the things that make for happy cats in this puzzle!

ADMIRATION

AFFECTION

BASKET

BED

BLANKET

CALM

CARE

CONTENTMENT

CUDDLES

CUSHION

FLOWER

FOOD

FOUNTAIN

GENTLENESS

HEALTH

HIDING PLACES

HOME

LOVE

PLAY

PURR

REST

SERENITY

STROKES

SUNSHINE

SWEET DREAMS

TOYS

TRANQUILITY

TREATS

WARMTH

WATER

```
A F F E C T I O N L O V E B T
K I C O N T E N T M E N T A R
J Q M L E N I H S N U S S O A
Y S Y O T A D E T W I E B D N
A D F W E G E M Y O C F M S Q
L N Y L M K M D L A I I L T U
P C X Y O K L O L S R A T R I
D R O U H Z Q P S A T E O O L
H J P E H U G E T Z K Y H K I
N K S E O N N I F N S O W E T
U A H E I E O Y A E C M O S Y
U P K D L N A L R F I Y J F K
H P I T A W B E K T F D M S X
X H N J X L N S N O I H S U C
M E S Z H I T X F L O W E R B
G C R M T F O O D T E K S A B
S N A Y A L L N W A O A W U D
S I N R Z E V L C A L M A L B
X D U I E R R S B A X J R Y L
T E J O A S E D E H R E M Z P
D B T W T T D T T L T F T P F
Q I S A E F N X A E D L H Y A
X Q E D F R X U A W E D A W O
E R R L R R U P O B U W U E M
T S Q Z T L V O H F E R S C H
```

Before and After

Both clues share the middle word. Example:

"Shoo!" – Nab   <u>S</u> CAT <u>C</u> <u>H</u>

1. Kathmandu's country – Ashen

___ ___ PAL ___ ___ ___

2. What kittens do – Cake tiers

___ LAY ___ ___ ___

3. Unexpected – Of teeth

___ ___ ___ DEN ___ ___ ___

4. Food on a skewer – Stubby tailed feline

___ ___ BOB ___ ___ ___ ___

5. Large brownish fruit – Hocked

___ ___ ___ PAW ___ ___ ___

6. Spotted wildcat – Moisturizer

___ ___ ___ LOT ___ ___ ___

7. Later meal – Long-haired breed

___ ___ ___ PER ___ ___ ___ ___

8. Buffed – Substratum

___ ___ ___ BED ___ ___ ___ ___

9. Show up – Premature

___ ___ ___ EAR ___ ___

10. Like many cats – Entry point

___ ___ DOOR ___ ___ ___

11. Comfortable – Iffy

___ ___ ___ TENT ___ ___ ___ ___ ___

Mew Math

Joanne's four cats, Biscuit, Ernie, Sophie, and Princess, all ate canned food. Biscuit ate 4 cans of food each day, while Ernie ate 3/4 as much. Both Sophie and Princess ate half as much as Biscuit. How many cans did Sophie and Princess eat?

Calling All Cats

As anyone with a cat in the house knows, one of her favorite places to lie is across a computer keyboard or on a cellphone. Now it happened that while Silver Streak was sleeping on a cellphone, she pressed:

6 – 9 – 7 – 8 – 3 – 7 – 4 – 6 – 8 – 7

The numbers happened to correspond with letters on the keypad that will complete this quote by novelist and poet Sir Walter Scott:

Cats are a

— — — — — — — — — —

kind of folk.

1	2 ABC	3 DEF
4 GHI	5 JKL	6 MNO
7 PQRS	8 TUV	9 WXYZ
*	0	#

That Cat

Answer each clue with two rhyming words – the title of this puzzle is an example! The number of spaces indicates the number of letters in each word.

1. Cat's favorite entrée, perhaps

   __ __ __ __   __ __ __ __ __

2. Cat scratcher

   __ __ __   __ __ __ __ __

3. Mama cat's coat

   __ __ __   __ __ __

4. Where cats sit in church

   __ __ __   __ __ __

5. Female cat given to tantrums

   __ __ __ __ __   __ __ __ __ __

6. Mama cat's day out minder

—— —— —— —— —— ——   —— —— —— —— —— ——

7. Striped overeater

—— —— —— —— —— ——   —— —— —— —— —— ——

8. Identically spotted cats

—— —— —— —— ——   —— —— —— —— —— ——

9. Light tomcat

—— —— —— ——   —— —— —— ——

10. Noise made when stalking

—— —— —— —— ——   —— —— —— —— —— ——

11. Only cat dish available

—— —— —— ——   —— —— —— ——

12. Catnip cousin clue

—— —— —— ——   —— —— —— ——

CATegories

While one cat eagerly greets you at the door, another cat plays hide-and-seek. Just the opposite! In Word Search 1, there are six cat traits; in Word Search 2, six antonyms. For a more challenging puzzle, cover the word box below!

Aloof	Finicky
Brave	Friendly
Calm	Restless
Domesticated	Subdued
Easygoing	Timid
Energetic	Wild

Cat Traits

```
G F T Y N X W V E C R L V A V J A
D J D I V A W L A H A D P H R L I
V K N K M W O L X Q E L Z B O V V
Q P S W E I M Q R T O F K O E K Z
X M K Y B C D P A C N G F B O M T
W T I C V I X C Q J M C O Z F C U
U Q U R J P I Z R B Q H M T Q I J
L K Z F J T Y F T J E C M T S U H
R T T O S H N H Y W Y K C I N I F
R V K E C C S F E V X M A Y C I O
U P M Z S W I H T N I J D U R P B
T O D J E J O E Z K P Q V F W S L
D J E N E R G E T I C E R R W R M
```

Antonyms

```
S H X L P Q C F M T Z C Y D L I W
U Q D U N N H Q F W L Z J W I I M
B U N E A S Y G O I N G K Y L F U
D K S J E H N R O M M U E E Q W D
U Q E C Q J Г Q Q J Ⅱ R F I E C ▪
E Y Z N S A T V R C Q A X U L W H
D L V T T S A M B R X S F I E T K
Q D Q P B E E L R U V A D V J N Q
Q N U X K Y G L Y Y X C E Y I R B
V E M Z M U P S T P M G M V D L P
Z I J O O C B Y X S F R E K A Y Z
A R K M N T L N M I E L L X Q R W
Y F Y Y A D G W L H W R X D W L B
```

CAT-Anagrams

Rearrange the letters in each word to create a word that is a synonym for the clue word!

1. TAME
   Partner: ___ ___ ___ ___

2. TREATS
   Potatoes: ___ ___ ___ ___ ___ ___

3. SERVAL
   Drool: ___ ___ ___ ___ ___ ___

4. LEAP
   Wan: ___ ___ ___ ___

5. NAPS
   Bridge: ___ ___ ___ ___

6. YARN
   Not: ___ ___ ___ ___

Cats and Dogs

A collector of cat and dog figurines found a small curio cabinet in a local antique shop. She brought it home, hung it on the wall of her rec room, and gathered 15 of her figurines to place in the cabinet's 12 slots. With only two clues, place the collector's figurines in the correct slots!

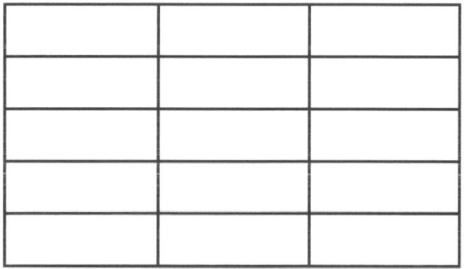

1. Once finished, the collector noticed that five cats formed a cross, vertically and horizontally, in the center of the cabinet.

2. No two dog figurines are together, either horizontally or vertically.

Animals are such agreeable friends –
they ask no questions, they pass no criticisms.
George Eliot

Cat in the Mirror

Unscramble these words, and then unscramble the circled letters to reveal what a fancy cat sees when she looks in the mirror!

O R R M A
⊕ _ ⊕ _ _

U S M O E
_ ⊕ ⊕ _ _

E S G U T
⊕ ⊕ _ ⊕ _

R A T S R Y
⊕ _ _ ⊕ _ _

E L T A P A
⊕ _ ⊕ _ _ _

Caption: __ __ __ __ __ __ __ __ !

Pampered

Answer each clue, and when you're done, the first letters of the words on the left and the last letters of the words on the right will spell out other words that cat fanciers use!

1. _ _ _ **P**

2. **A** _ _ _ _

3. _ _ _ **M**

4. **P** _ _ _ _ _

5. _ _ _ _ **E**

6. **R** _ _ _ _ _

7. **E** _ _

8. **D** _ _ _ _

1. Jump

2. Prize

3. Reproductive cell

4. "Good kitty!" and the like

5. Say

6. Eye part

7. First lady

8. Less bright

Kitty Comfort

As you make your way through this maze, pick up each toy and the basket in the middle will be full!

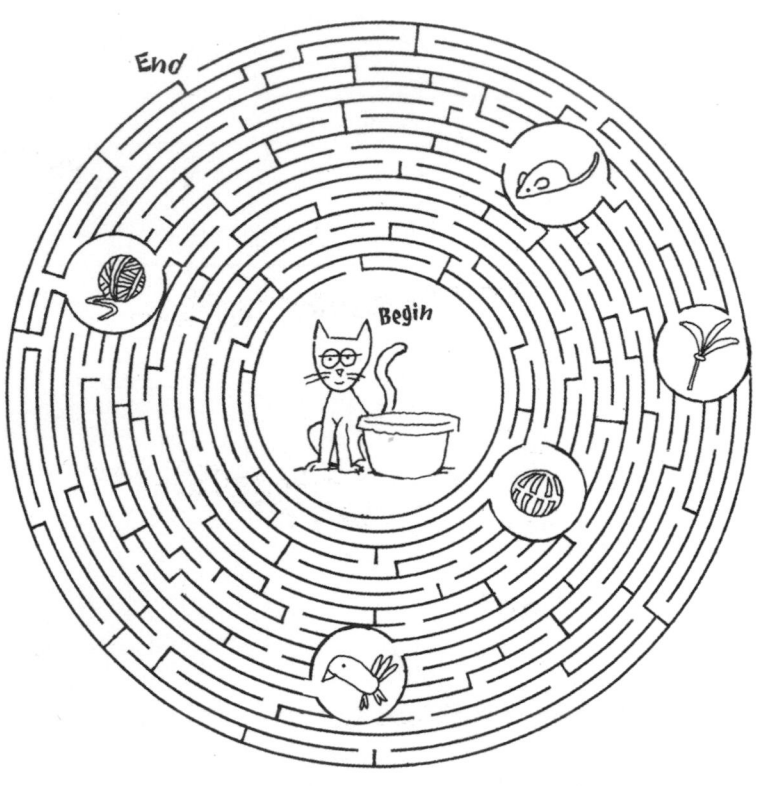

Zig-Zag Kittens

The playful kittens were chasing red, white, blue marbles from one end of the room to the other! Using the letters R, W, and B to stand for the colors, fill in the empty circles in such a way that no color is repeated in each line.

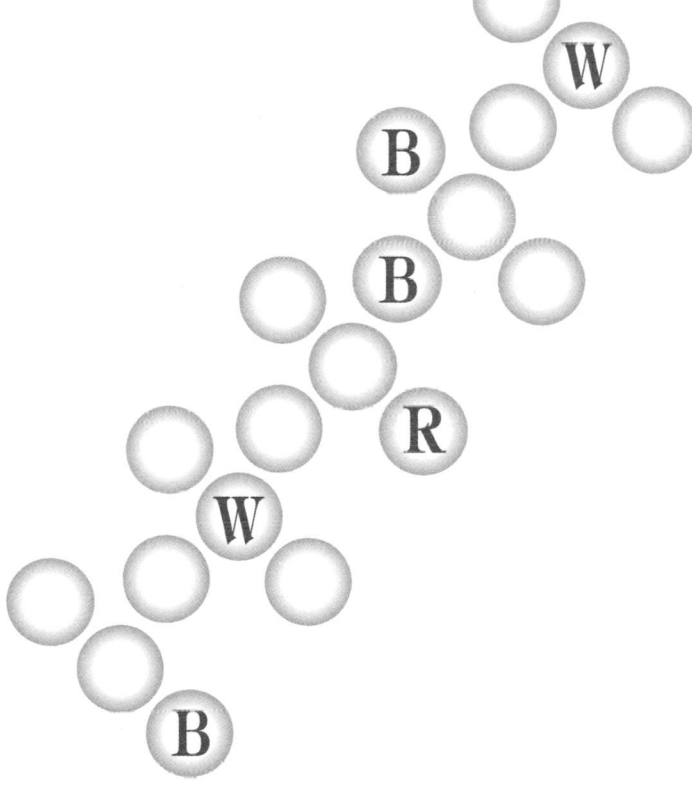

Cat's Cradle

Cats aren't noted for their willingness to follow directions, but if you do in this puzzle, the answer will reveal an alternative name!

Drop the letters down as you follow directions. The First one has been done for you.

1. Reverse the neighboring letters that spell "at."
2. In ninth place, <u>insert</u> an E.
3. Change the second vowel to a T.
4. Switch the first vowel and the R.
5. Change the third vowel to an R.
6. Change the second to last letter to an O.
7. Change the S to the third vowel in the alphabet.
8. Change the second vowel to the seventh letter in the alphabet.
9. Change the second C to an N.
10. Put a Y in twelfth place.
11. Substitute the first letter for an S.
12. Change the D to the letter that comes four letters from it in the alphabet.

	C	A	T	S	C	R	A	D	L	E		
1.	C	T	A	S	C	R	A	D	L	E		
2.												
3.												
4.												
5.												
6.												
7.												
8.												
0.												
10.												
11.												
12.												

Cat Connections

For each line of words, there is a single word that can be added to each to form a common compound word. The number of spaces indicates the number of letters in the answer.

Example: CALL, BOB, TAIL   <u>C</u> <u>A</u> <u>T</u>

1. FLAG, CAT, TAD   __ __ __ __

2. FUR, GAME, BUTTER   __ __ __ __

3. STRUCK, BEAM, HONEY   __ __ __ __

4. KID, KIN, CAT   __ __ __

5. MAN, IN, OUT   __ __ __ __

6. DRUM, PHONE, RING   __ __ __

7. RIGHT, CHILD, DAY   __ __ __ __ __

8. HOUSE, HOT, WOOD   __ __ __

9. BLUE, BLACK, RED ___ ___ ___ ___

10. CHAIR, BAND, UNDER ___ ___ ___

11. KEY, NOTE, FOOT ___ ___ ___

12. DO, BRAINED, BALL ___ ___ ___ ___

13. CLAW, BALL, LOOSE ___ ___ ___ ___

14. BRICK, FISH, SMITH ___ ___ ___

15. THING, PEN, HORSE ___ ___ ___ ___

16. CLOTH, WATER, PAN ___ ___ ___ ___

17. PILLOW, UPPER, CRANK ___ ___ ___ ___

18. SHOE, WARE, BALL ___ ___ ___ ___

19. OPENER, PIECE, PINK ___ ___ ___

20. TIP, HAMMER, NAIL ___ ___ ___

Building Blocks

A black cat and a white cat built a tower, taking turns adding a block. While the black cat's blocks were numbered, the white cat's blocks were blank. As the tower grew in height, a certain numbering sequence emerged. Fill in the white cat's blocks by deciphering the sequence!

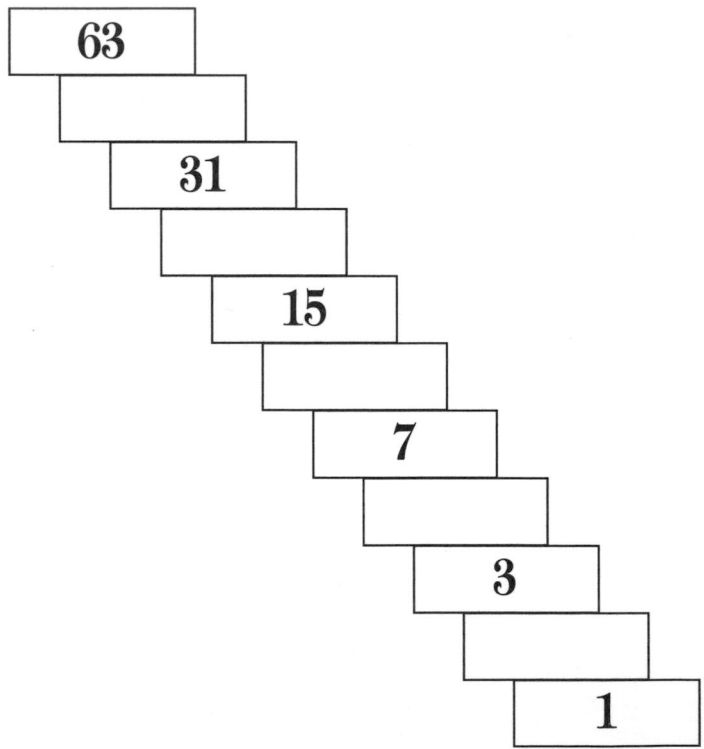

Bean Counter

Seems the kitten (read: dog did it) spilled the beans – a bag of beans! Each line of numbers stands for the number of beans in each pile. Look at the sequence, and enter the missing number!

1. 3   9   27   81 ___   729

2. 4   3   5   ___   6   5   7   6

3. 2   4   16   ___   65,536

4. 10   11   9   10   ___   9   7   8

5. 40   20   24   ___   16   8   12   6

6. 101   95   89   83   77   ___

There is no more intrepid explorer than a kitten.
Jules Champfleury

Stretch!

After a nice long nap, what's better than a kitty stretch? Each block in this s-t-r-e-t-c-h-e-d puzzle gets two letters!

ACROSS

3. How kitty gets her forever home
4. Male one
5. Cats' prey
6. Where the wild sand cat lives
7. Wild ferrets
9. Space between houses, often
10. What a dog will do, but not a cat, in general

DOWN

1. What cats have a lot of
2. Like catnip and other herbs
3. Vet's suggestion, perhaps
4. Cat with variegated coat with small or no white markings
5. Median
8. Tricolored cat that is almost always female

Palindromic Cats

A palindrome is a word or phrase that can be read either forward or backward, such as MOM. Each clue in this puzzle can be answered with a palindrome! The number of spaces indicates the number of letters in the answer. If you're stumped, pay attention to the clue word or words in italics.

1. An orange kitten is *ruddier* than his brother. The ruddier kitten could be called this compared to his brother:

(one word) __ __ __ __ __ __

2. Snowball hides behind the curtains and *glances out*. She like to:

(one word) __ __ __ __

3. Three cats are sitting on the porch steps. The white cat is on the bottom step, the black cat on the middle step, and the gray cat on the *uppermost* step. You might say that she has the:

(two words) __ __ __   __ __ __ __

4. *Littermates* Tammy and Tabitha are playing a game together. One says to the other: "I'm so glad you're my ___!"

(one word) ___ ___ ___

5. When Tabitha *scores the highest*, she exclaims to Tammy:

(three words) "___ ___ ___   ___   ___ ___ ___!"

6. A friendly *puppy* wants to play, too, but Tammy orders him away, saying:

(two words) "___ ___,   ___ ___ ___!"

7. In the kitchen, Callie sees that *Mama* possesses a certain cured pork meat. She observes:

(four words) "___ ___   ___ ___ ___   ___   ___ ___ ___!"

8. Callie is *crazy about* a certain *fish in the mackerel family*. She admits to being a:

(two words) ___ ___ ___ ___   ___ ___ ___

9. When the *tomcat* entered, a *kitten* said, "Hi,

(one word) ___ ___ ___!"

10. The bird wondered *if* he *had just seen a feline*, so he asked this question:

(6 words) ___ ___ ___   ___ ___   ___

___ ___ ___   ___   ___ ___ ___?

11. The feline, who's favorite food is a *filled and folded tortilla*, was called a:

(2 words) ___ ___ ___ ___   ___ ___ ___

12. When the feral cat's skin itched, he would find a *dry pod with stiff bristles* on it and *go up against* it. To relieve the itch, he would:

(2 words) ___ ___ ___   ___ ___ ___

Wild Cat Word Search

The comfortable cat curled up in your lap has many undomesticated cousins – and they're hiding someplace in this puzzle.

African Gold	Lion
Andean	Lynx
Asiatic Golden	Margay
Bobcat	Ocelot
Bornean Bay	Pampas
Caracal	Panther
Cheetah	Puma
Chinese Mountain	Sand Cat
Cougar	Serval
European Wildcat	Snow Leopard
Jaguar	Sunda Leopard
Jaguarundi	Tiger

```
D C L K M Y J S F F C G Y T S
E U A B U T V Q U B J T Q U M
C U D R O G Y L E J P U M A Q
S H R F A R Y N E G T B R N B
Z U I O Z C N F C S P G J Q Q
A I N N P B A E E O A T H Q T
S D E D E E O L A Y U H V I U
I N S G A S A B Z N L G G V R
A U N F P L E N C J B E A V X
T R O E O M E M W A R A O R A
I A W S O O B O O I T S Y W U
C U L P E C O H P U L M G J F
G G E W A R E C T A N D A I V
O A O E U M V L Q Y R T C W K
L J P N I J P A O U D D A A T
D A A A S A L A L T L U E I T
E C R E H G I U S O B I T T N
N Q D D W U O W G W R X P U Y
C J T N X A N N T A C D N A S
O A S A P R A H L B P M C R N
B S J S U C R I T P F S M L V
E M S P I I T K U F N N U M J
X D N R S C S V K F X R G D W
V X F X H L P M K N X N Y L Q
P A N T H E R O H A T E E H C
```

Transformations

Transform the top word into the bottom word by changing one letter at a time, with as few changes as possible.

Example: LOVE
D O V E
D O T E
D O T S
C O T S
CATS

1. FOOT

_____
_____
_____
_____
_____
_____

CLAW

2. PURR

_____
_____
_____
_____
_____

LICK

3. CURL

_____
_____
_____
_____
_____

SOFA

4. PLAY

_____
_____
_____
_____
_____

NAPS

5. FOOD

_____
_____
_____
_____
_____

DISH

6. COAT

_____
_____
_____
_____
_____

SKIN

7. HEAD

_____
_____
_____
_____
_____

TAIL

8. NOSE

_____
_____
_____
_____
_____

EARS

Cat Facts

How about those kitties? Choose the correct answer or, in some instances, answers.

1. How many teeth does a cat have?
    a. 20
    b. 30
    c. 40

2. Cats have 32 muscles in their:
    a. Ears
    b. Eyelids
    c. Jaw

3. A cat's whiskers help her to:
    a. Judge the size of openings
    b. Balance
    c. Sense shifts in air pressure

4. Very young kittens have no reaction to:
    a. Food
    b. Humans
    c. Catnip

5. A cat may purr when it's:
   a. Happy
   b. Stressed
   c. Ill

6. A tabby cat's distinctive forehead marking resembles the letter:
   a. M
   b. II
   c. W

7. On average, about how many hours each day do cats spend sleeping?
   a. 10
   b. 15
   c. 20

8. Cats, more so than humans, have better:
   a. Taste buds
   b. Night vision
   c. Computer skills

Forever Home

Adoption blesses a kitty with a forever home…
and blesses that home with a heart full of kitty love.
How many words of four letters or more can you form
by moving from one linked letter to the next? You may
move in any direction. You can go back to a letter, but
not stay on it for a double letter. No capitalized words
or plurals. We found 40 words!

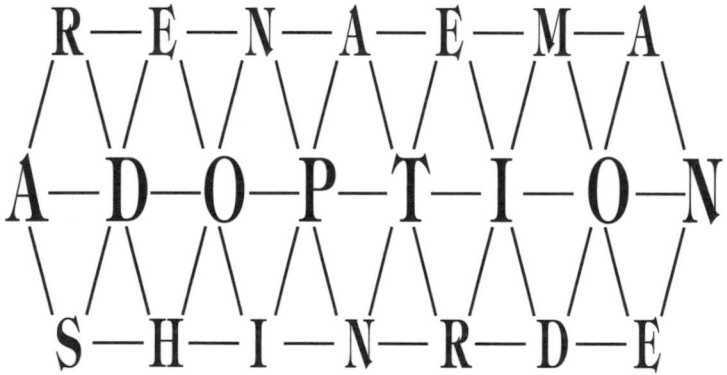

Heads and Tails

When a cat curls up to sleep, she can pull herself into a perfect circle! In this puzzle, the last two letters of the first answers form the first two letters of the second answer, and so on. The number of spaces indicate the number of letters in the answer.

1. What a cat likes to do after a long nap.

   — — — — — —

2. What a dog might do to a cat, or a cat to a mouse.

   — — — — —

3. Description of a poised, calm cat – or person.

   — — — — — —

4. What a cuddly cat likes to do in your arms.

   — — — — — —

5. "Last, but not" follower.

   — — — — —

6. Caress, as a cat.

__ __ __ __ __ __

7. Enclosure for a cat or dog.

__ __ __ __ __ __

8. Difficult to find.

__ __ __ __ __ __ __

9. Tuxedo cat's chest marking

__ __ __ __

10. Tabbys' marking, often.

__ __ __ __ __ __

11. Cat's bloodline.

__ __ __ __ __ __ __ __

12. How a cat's eyes look in the dark, sometimes.

__ __ __ __ __

Crypto-Cat

The words in each list are related to the caption. Determine the letter that each number stands for (the same code is used for all lists). Then, transfer the correct letter to the lines on the next page to reveal a cat-lover's sentiment! Hint: Find one answer, and begin to fill in. The first one has been done for you.

Cat Naps

C H A I R
10 5 7 11 17

__ __ __ __ __
12 7 21 11 2

__ __ __ __ __ __ __
10 3 9 5 11 2 14

__ __ __
19 11 14

__ __ __ __ __
9 5 16 8 18

__ __ __ __ __ __
10 8 2 9 16 21

Cat Treats

__ __ __ __
21 3 14 7

__ __ __ __ __ __ __
10 5 11 10 22 16 14

__ __ __ __
19 16 16 18

__ __ __ __ __
6 17 7 15 4

__ __ __ __ __ __
9 7 8 1 2 14

__ __ __ __ __ __
10 5 16 16 9 16

Cat Kinds

$\overline{9}\ \overline{11}\ \overline{7}\ \overline{1}\ \overline{16}\ \overline{9}\ \overline{16}$

$\overline{12}\ \overline{16}\ \overline{17}\ \overline{9}\ \overline{11}\ \overline{7}\ \overline{14}$

$\overline{17}\ \overline{7}\ \overline{6}\ \overline{20}\ \overline{2}\ \overline{8}\ \overline{8}$

$\overline{1}\ \overline{7}\ \overline{11}\ \overline{14}\ \overline{16}\quad \overline{10}\ \overline{2}\ \overline{2}\ \overline{14}$

$\overline{17}\ \overline{3}\ \overline{9}\ \overline{9}\ \overline{11}\ \overline{7}\ \overline{14}\quad \overline{19}\ \overline{8}\ \overline{3}\ \overline{16}$

Cat Toys

$\overline{18}\ \overline{2}\ \overline{11}\ \overline{8}\quad \overline{19}\ \overline{7}\ \overline{8}\ \overline{8}$

$\overline{18}\ \overline{16}\ \overline{7}\ \overline{21}\ \overline{5}\ \overline{16}\ \overline{17}$

$\overline{12}\ \overline{8}\ \overline{3}\ \overline{9}\ \overline{5}\quad \overline{1}\ \overline{2}\ \overline{3}\ \overline{9}\ \overline{16}$

$\overline{9}\ \overline{3}\ \overline{14}\ \overline{19}\ \overline{16}\ \overline{7}\ \overline{1}$

$\overline{17}\ \overline{2}\ \overline{8}\ \overline{8}\ \overline{11}\ \overline{14}\ \overline{6}\quad \overline{19}\ \overline{16}\ \overline{8}\ \overline{8}$

You're sure to agree that...

$$\overline{\underset{7}{}\ \underset{14}{}\ \underset{4}{}}\quad \overline{\underset{21}{}\ \underset{11}{}\ \underset{1}{}\ \underset{16}{}}\quad \overline{\underset{11}{}\ \underset{9}{}}\quad \overline{\underset{7}{}}$$

$$\overline{\underset{12}{}\ \underset{3}{}\ \underset{17}{}\ \underset{17}{}\ \underset{18}{}\ \underset{16}{}\ \underset{10}{}\ \underset{21}{}}\quad \overline{\underset{21}{}\ \underset{11}{}\ \underset{1}{}\ \underset{16}{}}$$

$$\overline{\underset{21}{}\ \underset{2}{}}\quad \overline{\underset{9}{}\ \underset{12}{}\ \underset{16}{}\ \underset{14}{}\ \underset{20}{}}\quad \overline{\underset{11}{}\ \underset{14}{}}$$

$$\overline{\underset{21}{}\ \underset{5}{}\ \underset{16}{}}\quad \overline{\underset{10}{}\ \underset{2}{}\ \underset{1}{}\ \underset{12}{}\ \underset{7}{}\ \underset{14}{}\ \underset{4}{}}\quad \overline{\underset{2}{}\ \underset{18}{}}$$

$$\overline{\underset{7}{}}\quad \overline{\underset{10}{}\ \underset{7}{}\ \underset{21}{}}!$$

Finicky Eaters

Five cats lived in Emma's home, and they were all finicky eaters! Every day, Emma set out five bowls, each with a different kind of cat food: fish paté, meaty paté, flaked salmon, chicken in gravy, and beef in gravy. As she prepared the food, there sat all five cats – Callie, Lady Gray, Ebony, Tom, and Snowball. Using the clues below, determine which cat headed to which bowl the moment Emma set them out.

1. Neither Tom nor Lady Gray could tolerate fish.
2. Snowball did not like paté.
3. Ebony preferred fish, but did not like flaked salmon.
4. Both Callie and Tom preferred gravy.
5. Callie did not like beef.

	Fish Pâté	Meaty Pâté	Flaked Salmon	Chicken in Gravy	Beef in Gravy
Callie					
Lady Gray					
Ebony					
Tom					
Snowball					

May I Come In?

The bolded words in this verse are anagrams of words in the Word Search. Enter the correct word in the space, and then find it in the puzzle below! The first one has been done for you.

```
A B M E D E R A P S G Y X B D X D
G T P E Q G V F F G F R S V E K O
G L I L F Z D U A G P E I W A D Z
A I J M E W B A I P B M Z T R S O
O B F W E A E V T Z E A K B Y T V
L E F Q W O S K V L A I T S U N Y
L S T W L L J E R P S N D S M T A
P T I Z Z O E R Q C T B Y O A A D
H V V G W E V Y X B S U S D H E B
G S X E R U S E L O T T L M E L L
O X M P I T E L L W E X Q J A C T
R T M P V O Z E Q Y X L I H R U B
E Z U A N N A G W D O T J U S T J
H V T J Y C N N Z V H S Y C O U K
N Y V T O Y Q A Y F H E Y D S O E
U F M U T P J E Z O S A U A W T S
E Z X N U N L F C I S L C Y W O U
V S J Y E I B L A X U M T B H A R
O P E V M N P R Z O D E T R E L A
L O L S Y L P Y G S G C A R E W N
```

I've been **related** ALERTED –
at **stale** _____ so I **hare** _____
that your home could **sue** _____ a cat –
Ton _____ **juts** _____ any old critter,
But the **bets** _____ of all **bastes** _____,
A **read** _____ and **volley** _____ cat!

Ruse _____, I'll need a few things
Like water and food –
Plus **nay** _____ treats you can **pears** _____
Tub _____ mostly I desire
Your **aspire** _____, **vole** _____, and **acre** _____.

An **glean** _____? **Toms** _____ of the **mite** _____!
My **sway** _____ can be **dowry** _____,
Yet I'll bring a **limes** _____ and happiness to your heart.
So, **yam** _____ I come in?
Say "yes," if you **asleep** _____
And you'll **marine** _____ a **hoer** _____ to me forever!

Insider Cat

Each answer word contains the word "cat." The number of spaces indi*cat*es the number of letters, and the bolded spaces show where the cat lies!

1. Kitty's trip to the beach, perhaps.

    — — — — — — — —

2. Artist's comic depiction of kitty.

    — — — — — — — — — —

3. What Tabby went to school to get.

    — — — — — — — —

4. Like the critical cat's derisive remark.

    — — — — — — — —

5. Grape variety…and kitty had fun when one rolled across the floor!

    — — — — — —

6. The cat that finished law school.

   — — — — — — — —.

7. When the vase fell down, what the cats did.

   — — — — — — — — —

8. A cat's nose helps to do this to food.

   — — — — — —

9. What the cat did by offering an ambiguous meow.

   — — — — — — — — — —

10. Perhaps Bach's cat helped him with this
    organ piccc in D minor.

    — — — — — — —

11. What the reigning cat did in favor of the heir.

    — — — — — — — —

12. A cat says "meow" to do this.

    — — — — — — — — — — —

Cat Tale

See if you can find all the cat-related words in the word box that are hiding in the following story!

There was a bag, a duffel, in Edinburgh, with her name on it. He marched back to the seats where she sat and said, "Mam, mallets are used with a marimba, lances are definitely not for this. Speaking of risky, of least possible safety, you should scrub this mad option for steel spears." "It's nonsense!" said the osprey loudly. "It's ironic – laws cover everything else."

ADOPTION	EARS	HISS
ARCHED	EATS	MAMMAL
BACK	FELINE	PREY
BALANCE	FLEAS	RUB
CLAWS	FRISKY	SENSE

```
I  I  K  X  Z  W  Q  S  T  M  W  G  B  K  M
V  D  Z  M  K  X  V  B  R  N  L  A  V  F  B
L  Y  B  Q  E  K  U  O  Z  E  L  J  I  Y  R
Y  S  L  X  V  R  F  D  G  A  W  U  K  O  E
A  Z  S  V  T  B  G  N  N  O  H  F  D  A  I
O  T  P  I  X  S  H  C  O  L  B  C  T  Z  Y
P  Q  J  G  H  E  E  V  Z  I  C  S  L  Q  N
I  V  K  B  X  Q  N  C  E  V  T  Z  P  F  R
W  K  R  U  P  O  V  K  C  C  C  P  R  P  A
Y  D  O  Z  R  D  N  M  P  Q  L  H  O  R  P
W  Q  C  O  C  Y  E  R  P  Q  P  T  C  D  T
J  T  M  D  S  A  W  J  J  F  C  H  L  E  A
D  V  S  I  L  S  N  A  M  U  E  M  E  O  Z
V  N  U  W  D  I  F  C  I  D  I  D  R  I  I
O  U  H  E  U  Z  M  C  B  L  W  T  U  K  N
B  W  O  W  A  K  N  A  C  I  K  G  B  V  C
J  L  S  B  C  O  C  S  Y  K  Y  I  Y  U  S
D  R  J  B  V  K  A  A  C  R  J  I  K  K  W
I  L  B  L  B  E  A  K  D  U  Q  B  S  X  P
L  E  V  H  L  H  Y  G  L  V  S  Q  I  A  N
A  N  O  F  Q  E  T  L  N  Z  R  U  R  V  O
M  I  I  Z  N  S  B  W  J  C  A  U  F  I  J
M  L  S  G  D  N  P  A  Z  G  E  L  E  Q  P
A  E  F  R  F  E  P  C  P  I  I  B  X  N  D
M  F  L  E  N  S  W  A  E  W  S  W  A  L  C
```

Fed Up?

Discover Dad's observation by choosing letters from the two lines. Letters are in order, reading left to right, but may come from either the first or second line. Enter your answers on the lines below.
Dad says:

L	O	A	K	A	S	I	K	N	R	O	E	
T	R	O	M	S	L	E	I	E	Y	R	U	
H	A	V	A	S	E	M	C	I	O	N	P	A
A	M	O	E	N	O	R	E	M	T	W	E	Y
I	T	A	H	A	T	I	A	T	Y			
L	N	T	R	E	K	N	T	O	N			

*Tabby swallowed
my quarter!*

_____ ____

___ ____ ____

_____ __ ___

_____!

Take Your Pick!

Take one letter from each of the four words to form an answer-word for the given clue.

Example:

L	E	N	D
S	O	C	K
A	I	M	S
M	U	T	T

Contented cat's demeanor: _C A L M_

O	P	T	S
M	U	S	E
C	H	I	T
L	A	N	D

1. An outdoor cat may be on it: _____

P	E	C	K
W	I	T	H
B	A	N	S
M	O	L	D

2. Cat scratcher: _____

C	R	E	W
B	A	Y	S
P	U	N	T
F	O	I	L

3. Cat's jump from place to place: _____

S	L	U	G
P	R	I	M
E	A	S	Y
M	U	T	E

4. Cat's tip: _____

S	U	E	T
M	A	K	E
B	I	R	D
C	H	O	P

5. Cat's insect irritant: _____

I	C	K	Y
C	O	S	T
F	A	D	S
T	H	E	N

6. Fat cat's regimen: _____

Cat Analogies

Select an answer to complete the second pair of words that most commonly fits the relationship suggested by the first pair of words.

1. Cat is to fish as _____ is to bone.
   a. Mouse   b. Dog   c. Kitten

2. Tabby is to tiger as _____ is to African wild dog.
   a. Doberman   b. Dachshund   c. Dalmatian

3. Bird is to cat as _____ is to dog.
   a. Bear   b. Goat   c. Squirrel

4. Barn cat is to mouser as _____ is to herder.
   a. Collie   b. Poodle   c. Chihuahua

5. Sphynx is to cat as _____ is to dog.
   a. Schnauzer   b. Mexican hairless   c. Wolf

A cat knows... sometimes the best thing to do is nothing at all.

There are 9 differences between these two pictures– can you find them all?

Flip-Flops

Kittens love to jump, roll, and flip sideways and upside down! In this puzzle, flip the first and last letters of the word that answers the first clue to get a word that answers the second clue. The number of spaces indicates the number of letters in the answer.

Example:

Look at a book : R E A D

Close to one's heart: D E A R

1. Group of sports players: __ __ __ __
   Cat food ingredient, often: __ __ __ __

2. What slit-eyed cat can do: __ __ __ __
   Possess forever: __ __ __ __

3. Young horse: __ __ __ __
   Stand around idly: __ __ __ __

4. Oolong and pekoe, e.g.: __ __ __ __
   Chair: __ __ __ __

5. Question word: __ __ __ __
   Defrost: __ __ __ __

6. Canvas cover, for short: __ __ __ __
   Role in show: __ __ __ __

7. Bosc, e.g.: __ __ __ __
   Harvest: __ __ __ __

8. Cadence in speech: __ __ __ __
   Plow: __ __ __ __

9. Implement: __ __ __ __
   Stolen goods: __ __ __ __

10. Emcee: __ __ __ __
    Utter nonsense in Britain: __ __ __ __

Mischievous Kittens

When Dolores returned home, she found her African violets on the floor, their potting soil spread across the room. Who did it? Each of her five kittens had a different story, but only one was telling the truth. Which one?

Tom: Patches did it.

Snowball: It was Patches, all right.

Luna: Yes, Patches.

Patches: Luna is lying.

Belle: Luna is telling the truth.

Who is telling the truth?

_____

Yet Dolores still didn't know which kitten was responsible for the upset flower pots, so she asked her four adult cats for their views. These are the answers she heard, and only one answer is the truth:

Mama: Mags is telling the truth.

Mags: I know who did it.

Biscuit: Mags doesn't know who did it.

Sam: Biscuit isn't telling the truth.

Who is telling the truth?

———————————————

One of the most striking differences between a cat and a lie is that a cat has only nine lives.

Whiskers the Housecat

Place each letter of the words "whiskers" and "housecat" in the empty boxes underneath each word to form a word of five or more consecutive letters reading left to right. Place every letter that appears in the word.

W H I S K E R S

A	R	E	A	T	E	R	O	S		E	E	P	S	A	K	E	N	D
N	O	T	E	M	A	N	I	C		C	L	E	R	D	I	N	G	S
C	L	A	S	L	E	N	G	T		E	T	E	D	O	U	T	I	N
L	I	T	G	R	O	C	O	A		T	E	R	N	A	L	I	N	G
I	N	C	H	T	O	M	A	R		I	V	A	L	O	R	T	O	N
E	S	B	E	A	U	N	T	H		A	R	T	F	H	O	R	G	E
P	I	N	E	C	S	E	C	R		T	H	E	N	Y	E	D	E	S
D	A	N	D	U	P	O	L	E		S	O	N	I	S	T	O	N	T

H O U S E C A T

M	E	S	T	E	S	C	A	T		E	R	D	O	O	R	O	O	M
E	N	T	R	O	A	T	A	M		T	E	U	R	U	E	D	U	E
V	O	L	O	N	T	E	E	M		S	I	C	I	S	T	H	E	R
P	R	I	M	E	N	I	N	C		I	N	G	A	R	Y	A	L	D
S	H	O	W	O	N	I	T	A		T	Y	E	T	I	N	G	S	O
R	I	T	H	O	U	L	D	E		O	D	D	L	E	T	I	N	G
A	W	A	N	E	O	S	P	O		K	Y	I	D	I	E	R	M	S
W	E	Y	E	S	T	E	R	L		A	D	E	R	M	U	N	D	E

Mama's Kittens

All four kittens in Mama Kitty's litter appeared to be the same weight, but in fact one kitten was lighter. Using a balance scale and no more than two tries, how could you determine which kitten was the lighter cat?

Cat-Word Puzzle

Place each of these words in the puzzle, crossing them off the list as you go. One answer has been added to get you started.

4 LETTERS
Bowl
Claw
Fish
Food
Hair
Hiss
Hunt
Jump
Meow
Paws
Play
Purr
Tail
Toys
Yarn

5 LETTERS
Bells
Breed
Loyal
Queen
Tabby

6 LETTERS
Catnip
Frisky
Kitten
Litter
Loving
Nature
Pretty
Stroke
Tomcat

7 LETTERS
Whisker

8 LETTERS
Friendly

9 LETTERS
Nine lives

NINE LIVES

Feline Definition Find

Find the definitions to the feline words in the word search grid!

1. Cat with more than the usual number of toes.

2. Cat with a distinctive forehead marking.

3. Tri-colored cat.

4. Self-sufficient; a cat's characteristic.

5. Cat breed with a spotted, wild-looking coat.

6. Cat's tooth.

7. Cat's favorite mint.

8. Housecat, vis-à-vis a wild cat.

9. Purebred cat's breed.

10. Spotted big cat native to Asia and Africa.

11. Big cat with jaws stronger than those of a lion.

12. Home claw-sharpener (2 words).

```
I  N  D  E  P  E  N  D  E  N  T  Z  S  J  J
U  R  C  F  X  M  F  S  D  V  S  J  L  C  A
D  L  S  D  C  Y  L  G  T  R  D  S  H  V  G
P  I  R  J  O  A  M  G  U  W  L  Y  T  F  U
E  K  V  N  O  J  L  V  Y  E  Q  B  N  O  A
D  D  G  E  I  T  Q  I  O  L  K  Q  H  P  R
I  S  L  Y  H  S  M  P  C  O  O  W  B  Y  N
G  R  B  O  O  Q  A  B  V  O  H  A  L  I  P
R  L  R  R  U  R  K  S  M  M  M  Y  B  D  I
E  N  F  T  D  X  D  K  Z  L  P  C  E  F  B
E  R  O  W  X  R  P  V  L  A  N  S  O  J  J
Z  I  J  Q  U  M  P  Y  M  O  T  T  R  H  T
I  W  C  M  N  Z  X  W  R  V  F  E  A  S
C  E  I  T  C  L  K  L  T  A  B  B  Y  W  O
A  N  T  F  L  D  B  L  M  X  D  H  X  I  P
T  J  S  V  E  Y  R  X  Y  Q  L  J  N  D  G
N  G  E  H  F  X  M  Y  E  Y  P  E  J  N  N
I  J  M  K  N  G  U  U  T  A  S  Q  Z  Q  I
P  A  O  H  N  I  X  C  V  C  V  X  M  G  H
V  S  D  A  D  N  A  R  Z  P  I  Z  Y  L  C
U  H  F  P  F  D  M  T  S  E  W  G  C  A  T
L  D  V  A  Y  C  K  L  G  I  V  H  V  G  A
X  C  L  L  J  V  K  P  D  S  X  E  I  N  R
X  O  O  Z  Q  S  N  O  C  A  A  M  O  E  C
R  P  G  O  D  U  C  Y  P  K  V  W  D  B  S
```

Droplets

Drop the letters into their respective column to reveal a cat-centric proverb! The first line has been done for you. Note: The end of the line does not mean the end of a word.

J	U	U	~~A~~	L
S	N	~~C~~	A	A
I	B	O	S	L
E	I	O	F	~~T~~
~~A~~	M	N	G	H
E	I	S	L	
L	S	A	N	
A		C	A	T

Word Analogies

Based on the relationship between the first word pair, complete the second word pair.

1. Cat – Feline
   Turtle – _____

2. Bees – Swarm
   Cats – _____

3. Claw – Paw
   Nail – _____

4. Sniff – Scent
   Taste – _____

5. Chair – House
   Pew – _____

6. Purr – Contentment
   Smile – _____

Cat Walk

Each number stands for a letter. Once you identify the code used, you can easily decipher this observation by nineteenth century novelist and feline fancier Jules Verne!

— —— —— ——, —— —— ——
1   2 1 3   4   1 5

—— —— —— ——,   —— —— —— —— ——
6 7 8 9   2 10 7 11 12

—— —— —— ——   —— ——   ——
13 1 11 14   10 15   1

—— —— —— —— ——   —— —— —— —— —— —— ——
2 11 10 7 12   13 4 3 16 10 7 3

—— —— —— —— —— ——
2 10 5 4 15 17

—— —— —— —— —— —— ——.
3 16 8 10 7 17 16

Domestic Cats

There's a kitty hiding in each sentence. Can you spot each one?

1. He thought, the cut was caused by a fang or a claw.

2. "Send a wire! Hair-raising things are happening!" he shouted.

3. "Pick up the tab," bystanders laughed.

4. "The cat's in that tree?" she asked. "Jeepers!" I answered.

5. Oh, man, x-rays cinched the diagnosis.

6. She went out looking like a ragamuffin.

7. In the snow, shoes are mandatory.

Kitty's Bedtime Prayer

Find the bolded words in this word search puzzle.

Now I **lay** me down to **sleep**,
I pray this **cushy** life to **keep**.
I pray for **toys** that look like **mice**,
And **sofa** cushions **soft** and nice.
For **grocery bags** where one can **hide**,
Just like a **tiger**, crouched inside!
I pray for **gourmet** kitty **snacks**,
And **someone** nice to **scratch** my **back**.
For **window sills** all **warm** and **bright**,
For **shadows** to **explore** at **night**.
I pray I'll always **stay** real **cool,**
And keep the **secret feline** rule
To **never** tell a **human** that
The **world** is really **ruled** by cats!

```
Y U J G E C Q R N V X H A J U
N Z B F A H C T A R C S U X W
Z G R O C E R Y B A G S L A A
P W O R L D K O N D O E R B L
U P G X Z U I G H P X M U A S
P T T U J M Q A A P P D Y Q O
S E C R E T F E L I N E O A U
M K C H B P B O S W O D A H S
R M S I A M R X Y E I K A W Z
U Z T L M E T Z J D S O D O J
L X A F C B S T M D F L E B G
E V Y A T R Q E P E E L S X M
D U G L V I K D B A C K S O F
W T K O N G C F C U S H Y N L
I X H Q F H P J Q L R T A S Z
N Y B Z V T S Q Q O R M B T V
D C S Y V I D X W E U Q L D E
O Q O K K E E P V H J R E W I
W I F L T D F E E N O E M O S
S T T M I E N J B S O E V W B
I T P H K L M R Q U K W Y V S
L H L Q A P H R E E S C X H B
L G F O C F Z G U G P Y A L M
S I C Q O Y O D Z O I H O N W
G N B Z H C C S O X G T M T S
```

Mew Math

Three kittens were playing in the yard when a puppy entered and wanted to join the fun. Unfortunately, the kittens would have nothing of it! The first kitten ran to hide in a hedge 15 feet away. The second kitten scampered back into the house, which was twice as far. The third darted into a neighbor's yard, which was half again as far as the other two cats' distances combined. How far did the third kitten travel?

Word Play

What's unique about each of the following words or phrases?

1. Was it a cat I saw?

2. Meow, Growl, Purr

3. Fluffy's fur flew five feet, Freddy!

4. Listen/Silent, Rescue/Secure, Meals/Males

5. Calico, Tiger, Camel, Robin

"A" Crossword Addition

There's someone special "sitting" in the middle of this puzzle!

ACROSS

1. Dickens' Tiny __
4. Dad's mate
7. Recline
8. Victorian was one
9. Encompassed
11. [?]
12. Usual
16. Atmosphere
17. Like every day
18. Layer
19. "Golly"

DOWN

1. Kindly solicitude, for short
2. Sundial number
3. Planet
4. What a snowman is doing in spring
5. Miner's find
6. Angry
10. [?]
12. Knock
13. Frying need
14. Born
15. Sheep bearer

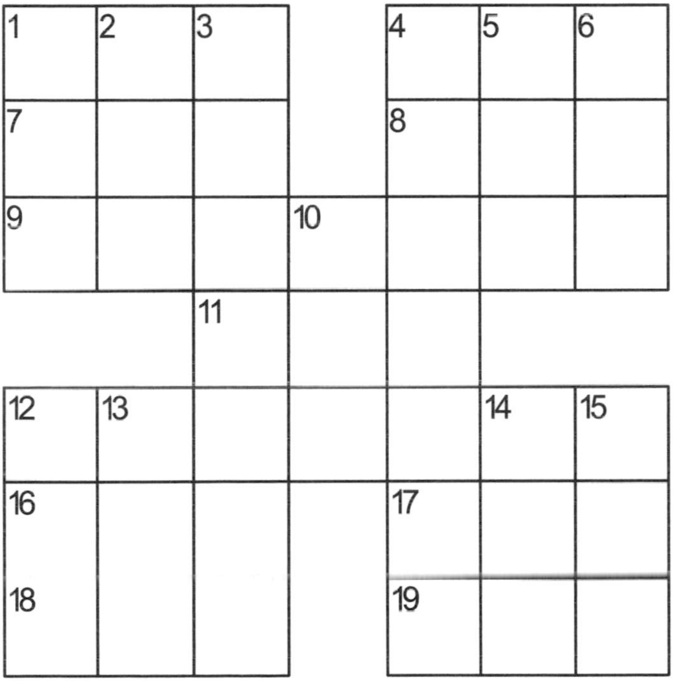
1 2 3
4 5 6
7
8
9
10
11
12 13
14 15
16
17
18
19

Sweet Name

By moving from one linked letter to another, spell out a 9-letter word that would be a sweet name for a cat of a certain color. You may return to an adjacent letter, but not stay on a letter.

— — — — — — — — —

Mew Math

A veterinarian needs exactly 9 oz. of water to mix with a cat's food supplement. However, she has only a 7 oz., 8 oz., and 10 oz. container. How can she fill the 10 oz. container with exactly 9 oz. of water?

Cat Attractions

The names of three kitty-attracting items are hidden in each line of letters. Pick and cross off one letter from each box going across left to right to form one four-letter word; then go back and cross off another letter from each box to form another; and then again until you have found all three. One letter of each word will not be used.

1.	**SLAB**	**ALOE**	**FAIL**	**HALF**
2.	**DEFT**	**OBOE**	**BOYS**	**SKID**
3.	**STUB**	**ARIA**	**RENT**	**DEED**

1. _____ _____ _____

2. _____ _____ _____

3. _____ _____ _____

Mew-sery Rhyme

This is a classic English nursery rhyme and riddle. Can you come up with the correct answer'?

As I was going to St. Ives,
I met a man with seven wives.
Each wife had seven sacks.
Each sack had seven cats.
Each cat had seven kits.
Kits, cats, sacks, wives…

How many were going to St. Ives?

Forever Home

Each word in this list has a place in kitty's forever home. To get you started, FOREVER HOME has been entered!

4 LETTERS
- Care
- Dish
- Food
- Love
- Play
- Rest
- Toys

5 LETTERS
- Cream
- Sleep
- Water

6 LETTERS
- Basket
- Catnip
- Litter
- Treats
- Window

7 LETTERS
- Blanket
- Comfort
- Cuddles
- Feather
- Pillows

8 LETTERS
- Brushing
- Sunshine

F
O
R
E
V
E
R
H
O
M
E

105

What's In a Name?

A group of cat-lovers decided to form a club. When the roster was complete, the club's leader noticed something interesting about the names of members. What was it?

Carol

Ginger

Holly

Noel

Opal

Robin

Rose

Pedigree Cats

Take groups of letters from columns A, B, and C (in that order) to complete the name of a popular breed of cat. The first one is done for you.

A	B	C	
~~PE~~	SSI	LUE	PERSIAN
BU	NG	~~AN~~	_____
HIM	NEC	SE	_____
BE	AM	YAN	_____
RUSS	~~RSI~~	NIAN	_____
SI	RME	AN	_____
ABY	IANB	ESE	_____
RA	RM	OON	_____
BI	ALA	LL	_____
MAI	GDO	AL	_____

Cat Food Cubicle

You've received a big delivery of cat food! You decide to arrange the cans in a cubicle divided into three rows and three columns. In addition, you want each row and column to contain exactly 15 cans, with no repeated number throughout the grid. Using the numbers 1 through 9, how could you do this?

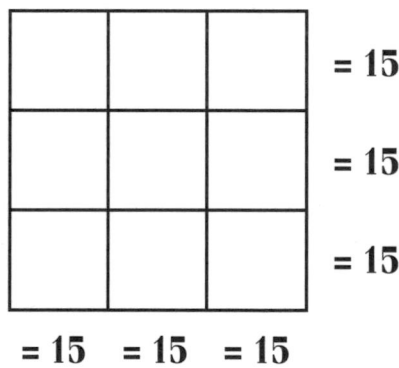

Cans of Cat Food

A friend has arranged 10 cans of cat food in a triangle. You are challenged to invert the triangle by moving only three cans. How can you do this?

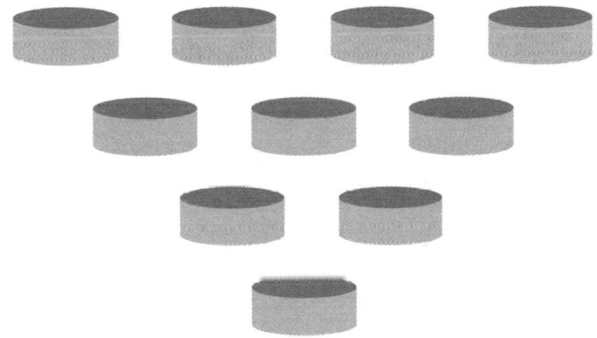

Crowded Crossword

Place two or three letters in each block. The words are arranged according to the number of blocks they will fill. Words may read across left to right or down. One entry has been made to get you started.

			███	
███		███		
		███		███
		FUR		███
███		NISH	███	
		ED	███	
	███	███		

2 BOXES	FURRY	**3 BOXES**
ABLE	MOUSER	AMIABLE
ACED	NINE	~~FURNISHED~~
FINDER	ORATE	ORDERED
FINNISH	POSER	POETRY
		SCRAMBLE
		SUNSHINE

Purr-fect Family

Mama Cat's five kittens were ready for adoption. Her human, Judy, had two friends, Marilyn and Jerry, and one neighbor, Lois, who were interested. She invited them over one afternoon to visit the kitties. At the end of the afternoon, one person left with two kittens, the other two visitors took one each, and Judy decided to keep one, along with Mama. From the clues below, place each kitten in its new home.

1. Jerry did not choose a male kitten.
2. Judy kept one of the toms.
3. Lois was interested in both the white and the orange kittens, but could take only one.
4. The orange kitten went home with one of Judy's friends.

	Gray female	Gray tom	White female	Black female	Orange tom
Judy					
Marilyn					
Jerry					
Lois					

Contrary Cats

When on one side of a closed door, a cat wants to be on the other side! To solve this puzzle, unscramble each set of letters to form a pair of antonyms. You may be able to form more than one word from a particular letter combination, but only one choice will give you the correct, "contrary" answer. The first one has been done for you.

1. RACECS   – MOONMC
    SCARCE   – *COMMON*

2. TUNEI   – DIDEVI
        –

3. LATOF   – KINS
        –

4. SIREA   – RELWO
        –

5. RHSEF   – LASET
        –

6. SPERIA   – MLABE

  _____   –   _____

7. PAXNED   – TTCCRNOA

  _____   –   _____

8. EOSLC   – AIDTNTS

  _____   –   _____

9. DRIPA   – GIGSSHUL

  _____   –   _____

10. NRIEN   – TRUEO

  _____   –   _____

11. DREU   – PETOLI

  _____   –   _____

12. EENINTL   – TTSCRI

  _____   –   _____

Go-Togethers

In each row of four words, one word is out of place. Which one?

1. Bengal, Spaniel, Snowshoe, Maine Coon

2. Fillets, Milk, Paté, Shreds

3. Peppermint, Spearmint, Parsley, Catnip

4. Mediterranean, Veterinarian, Vegetarian, Vegan

Cutest Cat Competition

Members of the Kitty Cat Club decided to award prizes to human counterparts of the three cutest cats in the club. For the event, club president Amanda prepared three envelopes. First Prize, a $50 gift card; Second Prize, a $35 gift card; and Third Prize, a $25 gift card. But after the envelopes were sealed, she realized that all three were mislabeled. By opening only one envelope, she correctly labeled each one. How did she do it?

Paw-sibilities

Choose the correct definition to these cat-related words!

1. A feral cat is:
   a. Wild   b. Domesticated   c. Tame

2. An ailurophile is one who:
   a. Loves cats   b. Fears cats   c. Is allergic
                                         to cats

3. A caterwauling cat is:
   a. Purring   b. Nursing   c. Howling

4. A polydactyl cat has more than the usual number of:
   a. Toes   b. Teeth   c. Paws

5. Cats have retractable:
   a. Paws   b. Claws   c. Tails

6. Cats, along with other mammals, have a third:
   a. Kidney   b. Stomach   c. Eyelid

7. A Sphynx cat is known for its:
   a. Noble   b. Lack of hair   c. Size
   bearing

8. A tuxedo cat is:
   a. Bicolored   b. Tricolored   c. Black or white

9. Most male tortoiseshell cats are:
   a. Spayed   b. Neutered   c. Sterile

10. The largest of these three cats is a:
   a. Tiger   b. Panther   c. Cheetahs

"Only" a Cat!

Find the bolded words in the word search.

I'm only a **cat**
And I **stay** in my **place** –
Up **there** in your **chair**,
On your **bed**, or your **face**!

I'm **only** a cat
And not **finicky** – **much** –
Like, I'm **happy** with **cream**
And **salmon** and **such**!

I'm only a cat,
And we'll get **along** fine,
As **long** as you **know**
I'm not **yours**…you're all **mine**!

```
Y H N F K W W G O B S T A Y W
H F P A G P N Q I B E Q B A M
O Z Y N R R P T P F O D G P C
Y S O J S S T G N O L A D X L
Y T U S I P C T F D I Z X T C
V X R O T G C U Z R J G G H N
M Q S I R N A X H J Z U A F B
J X A V Y C E R E H T I D G S
X K Z W K R R L N C R L V U S
U C W L B F I E M Q P Y C Q V
C U H I V G M U A H H H D Y P
H W Q K O E T A C M G W V B N
W X C E P F W Q H F H L X S G
Y A D E O O L Y W R E G B S X
H S A J N R K M X N U X P M H
H I S K C C W K B O Z M V D
J Q A S I C H J G A L M T X R
E W T N K A M E E C M M L U Q
D K I Q A W G M Q I C X C A F
X F L W Q H S T N D A N R W S
E J J W I O A E R F Y G B Z B
C H T C J Y X Y A P P P N B A
A I C V B L V C P U T X Z O Q
L I A U Z T E A Y Y L N O B L
P A F A M F H R G H B T D H H
```

Cats in the Crossword

There are a couple catty answers in this puzzle!

ACROSS

1. Not on shore
5. Wide-eyed cat's eyes, e.g.
9. Like a white cat in France
11. Former European currency
12. __ Rica
13. Tie score
14. Part of a business address, maybe (Abbr.)
15. Fro's partner
17. Wide shoe size
18. Release
20. Selection
22. Ace
23. 3.14
24. Series ender (Abbr.)
27. Unattractive
29. South Pacific island
31. For the __ of (motive)
32. Noise in the night, sometimes
33. Rhymes with kitty's favorite pastime
34. "Understood" (Two words)

DOWN

1. Basics
2. Opening, as for mail
3. What cats take, with "their..."
4. Colony inhabitant
5. Stadium cheer
6. Torn apart
7. Angora, for example
8. Reasonable
10. Cat treat
16. Double-reed instrument player
18. Salt Lake City's state (Abbr.)
19. What a cat wants when outside a closed door
20. Church instrument
21. Folk dance
22. Cat moniker
24. Ostrich relatives
25. Big book
26. __ of Good Hope
28. "Sure!"
30. Large tuna

Changes

Follow the directions to solve this puzzle!

1. Add a letter to the word SLEEP and rearrange to form a word meaning "to satisfy."

   —— —— —— —— —— ——

2. Change one letter in the word CLOWDER to form the name of a creamy stew.

   —— —— —— —— —— —— ——

3. Change two letters in the word QUEEN to form a noun synonymous with "hunt" or "expedition."

   —— —— —— —— ——

4. Add a letter to the word TOM and rearrange to form the name of something that encircled medieval castles.

   —— —— —— ——

5. Drop a letter from the word BENGAL and rearrange to form a word meaning "to gather."

   —— —— —— —— ——

6. Change a letter in the word CLAW to name a kind of salad.

___ ___ ___ ___

7. Add a letter to the word YOWL and rearrange to form a word that means "humble."

___ ___ ___ ___ ___

8. Drop three letters from the word STRIPES and find a word that is a synonym for "excursion."

___ ___ ___ ___

9. Drop one letter from ANGORA and rearrange to form a word that means "grumble" or "whine."

___ ___ ___ ___ ___

10. Drop one letter from the word BASKET and rearrange to form the name of something you might do on ice.

___ ___ ___ ___ ___

Purr-fect Placement

Arrange these words in the grid below so that you have common five-letter words reading across and down. One word has been inserted to get you started.

ATOLL	CASES	SLOTS
ATONE	ELECT	SODAS
CARET	ENACT	~~TESTS~~
	RODEO	

				T
				E
				S
				T
				S

A Cat Lives Here

In the letter scramble to the right is hidden the phrase "Furry ball" from the poem below, can you spot it?

Furry ball
Of warmth and grace,
Amber eyes
On whiskered face.
Zany larks,
Frenzied glare—
Languid prowl
To comfy chair.
Hear the purr?
Me-ew, me-ew!
There's a cat
At home with you!

F R U R Y L A B L F R
U R Y L A B L F R U R
Y L A B L F R U R Y L
A B L F R U R Y L A B
L F R U R Y L A B L F
R U R Y L A B L L R U
R Y L A B L F A U R Y
L A B L F R B R Y L A
B L F R U Y Y L A B L
F R U R R L A B L F R
U R Y R A B L F R U R
Y L U B L F R U R Y L
F F U R Y L A B L F R
U F Y L A B L F R U R
Y L A B L F R U R Y L
A B L F R U R Y L A B
L F R U R Y L A B L F
R U R Y L A B L F R U
R Y L A B L F R U R Y
L A B L F R U R Y L A
B L F R U R Y L A B L
F R U R Y L A B L F R

Cat Crossings

Follow the directions, and when you're finished, read a quotation by American author and educator William Lyon Phelps.

1. Cross out all colors.
2. In columns A and D, cross out all words with double letters.
3. Cross out all words that end in O.
4. Cross out all words that contain the word EAT.
5. In columns B and C, cross out all words containing OU.
6. Cross out all names of flowers.
7. Cross out all containers.
8. Cross out all numbers.
9. Cross out all words that rhyme with LOOK.
10. Cross out all words that contain the word LINE.
11. Cross out all six-letter words that could be divided into two three-letter words.
12. Cross out all words that are anagrams of the word NOTES.

Quote: _____

_____

A	B	C	D
TREAT	BOOK	A	FELINE
ROSE	ORANGE	SHOUT	INNER
ECHO	CAT	BOXES	DAHLIA
MAGENTA	ENOUGH	ONSET	POURS
TEN	ASTER	FOUR	BENEATH
CHEETAH	INLINE	BOO-BOO	OUTLINES
LINER	REPEAT	BOBCAT	BIN
HIS	DEFEAT	GRAY	ANYWAY
MOON	CAN	OUTDOORS	FEELING
THREE	BODY	TOOK	BETTER
RED	BOWL	ON	SIX
HOOK	AMBER	EYELID	CAMELLIA
THE	ONE	GERANIUM	GLOOM
HAPPY	CALICO	POUT	BIGWIG
STONE	FLOOR	HEATH	BLUE
DAISY	OUTRUN	RECLINER	SILO
LIKE	THOROUGH	TONES	SIX
OTTER	DECLINE	WATER	WILL

When God Made Cats

Find each bolded word in the word search grid!

When God made **cats**,
He **used** the **graceful**
waving of the **grass**,
The **gentle** murmur of the river
as its **waters** pass.
The **happy** flight of **butterflies**
that dart among the **flowers**,
The peaceful, **dreamy** quality
of **quiet** nighttime **hours**.

When God **made** cats,
He took the **warmth**
of **sunshine** in the **spring**,
The **bright** and **joyful** sound of **robins**
as they **chirp** and **sing**.
He added **love** and faithfulness
through all the **nights** and **days**,
And made a creature who is **simply**
purrfect in all **ways**!

```
H O U R S W X F R Y L P M I S
N I G H T S K D B O M H H P J
K Y W Z J R Z A Y P S I P S H
E C S N T V N S U Z U O Q P H
E F W T G P L T H G I R B R G
E L O L A J L B Y H P M C I R
Z O H Q E C L O V E T G M N E
I W K J Q S N I B O R M W G I
F E D S X K W C Y N D P R L E
W R I D Y B N P R M D C A A W
B S A Z E A P T P O A O Z Q W
G E W A Y A D Q H W F E G U S
I R C K H B V D C A Y L R I N
I D A Y T V O Z J Y A K N D M
T A S C X C U Y E S Z G S A W
R X S B E S E Q X V C E O V U
E Y R W E F Z F E M I B O A N
I P E D Q T U N R L E D A M U
Y R T O Z B I L F R J J V S U
Z I A O T H E R L L U B E G I
G H W G S L E H U Q T P J R H
Y C O N T T A F C U N E J P H
K E U N T W Y W T B E W I J X
T S E U F O S S A R G U M U U
J G B F J Y J M U F D X T U Q
```

Letter Drop

When the letters are arranged correctly in each column, an astute observation by French poet Francois Joseph Méry is revealed! The word has been done for you. Note: The end of the line does not mean the end of a word.

A	A	D		E	~~A~~	C
~~E~~		E	E	~~M~~		~~D~~
E	F		E	M		G
G	I	G		O	A	L
	I	H	G		A	N
I	O	N	H	R	E	
K	T		S	R	P	O
O	T	S	T		R	
T	V	T	U	T		
				M	A	D
E						

Mew Math

Each of the calico's three female kittens had one brother. How many kittens were in the calico's litter?

All Kinds of Cats!

Fill in the grid with words from this list of cat breeds. One entry has been made to get you started.

6 LETTERS
Angora
Bengal
Birman
Bombay
Exotic
Ocicat
Sphynx

7 LETTERS
Bobtail
Burmese
Persian
Ragdoll
Siamese

8 LETTERS
Devon Rex
Munchkin
Siberian
Snowshoe

9 LETTERS
Chartreux
Himalayan
Maine Coon

17 LETTERS
American Shorthair

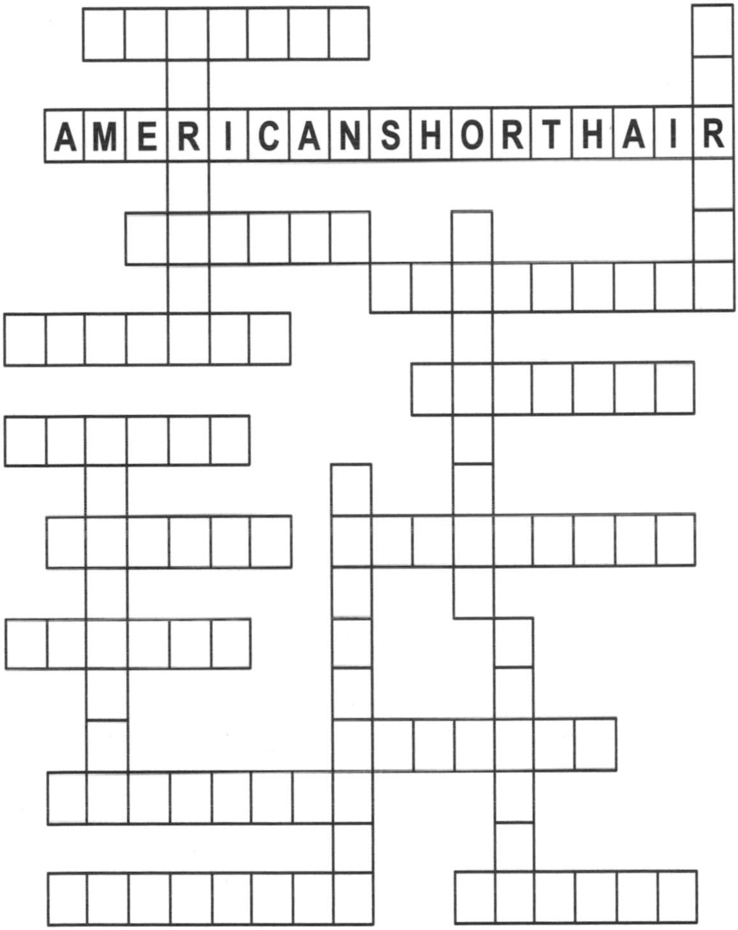
AMERICANSHORTHAIR

Drop-a-Letter

Drop one letter and rearrange the rest to answer the clues!

1. MOUSER -   The tomcat hoped the sleeping mouse wouldn't do this as he approached.

   _____

2. LEOPARD -   Supervised, conditional release for the big cat who promised to change his spots.

   _____

3. PERSIAN -   The fluffy feline leaps from a ladder and gets one.

   _____

4. SERVAL -   The enthusiastic wild cat's high praises for his tasty meal.

   _____

5. SOMALI -   What the farm cat walked on as he crossed the fertile fields.

   _____

Oh, Those Kittens!

Unscramble the words, and then unscramble the circled letters to find out why, when one kitten climbed a tree, all her littermates followed.

I T T S P Y

__ ◯ __ __ ◯ __

C O O P L I T

◯ __ __ __ ◯ __

A P E V I R T

◯ __ __ ◯ __ __

T E C A N C

__ __ ◯ __ ◯

Because they're __ __ __ __ __ __ __ __ !

JIGSAW

Each letter combination fits someplace in the grid! There's a clue for each row, and each answer will have six letters.

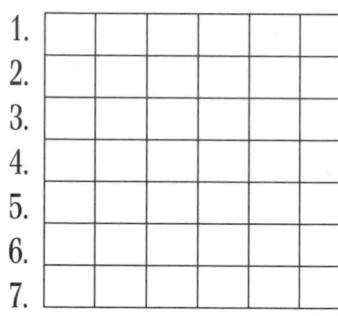

1. Cat's favorite mint
2. Jump
3. It's usually a female cat
4. Partner for #3
5. Tabby feature
6. Happy cat makers
7. Like kittens

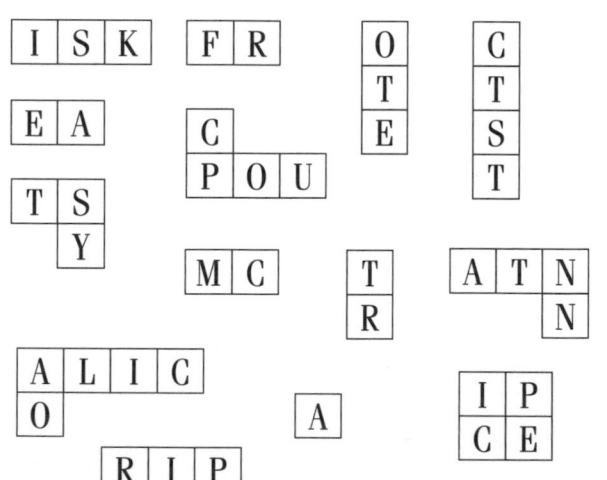

Six Cats

Fill in the middle line of each set with a word that forms two compound words using the first and middle word, and the middle and third word.

Example: Any ___HOW___ Ever

1. Cat _____ Time

2. Cat _____ Box

3. Catch _____ Side

4. Cat _____ Way

5. Catch _____ Smith

6. Cat _____ Bone

Kitty Collectibles

All her friends know that Eloise loves cats, so she has received many "catty" gifts through the years! She keeps them in a curio cabinet. From the clues, can you figure out how she has arranged them? "Left" and "right" refer to the viewpoint of one looking at the cabinet.

1. All the figurines are ceramic, except those on the bottom row, which are made of fabric (2), straw (1), and yarn (2).
2. All the Christmas-themed cats are on the top row. A cat with holly is on the far left, and a cat with a Christmas tree is on the far right. Between them are two angel cats and one cat ornament.
3. She has collected nine large figurines and five small figurines.
4. Eloise was given a plaque with a cat poem on it, which she put in the center of the display. A large figurine and a straw cat sit in the boxes below the plaque.
5. The two angel cats are placed to the left of the cat ornament.
6. Fabric cats sit in opposite corners.

7. Large cats have been placed directly above both yarn cats.
8. Four large cats complete the row with the plaque.
9. Small cats are directly below both angel cats, and at the opposite ends of the row with three large cats.
10. A small cat sits on the shelf below the cat with the Christmas tree.

Eloise's Kitty Collection

Cat Blocks

Arrange the given words in each block, reading left to right, so that new words form reading top to bottom. The words in the shaded squares are cat-centric!

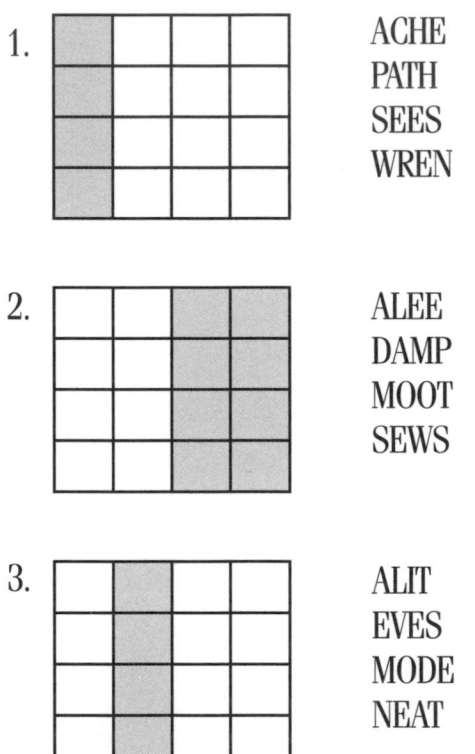

1. ACHE
    PATH
    SEES
    WREN

2. ALEE
    DAMP
    MOOT
    SEWS

3. ALIT
    EVES
    MODE
    NEAT

Are You Kitten Me?

Shakespeare's cat had a question. Unscramble the words, and then read the circled letters from left to right to reveal what it was!

A A A A M R C N T

U Y S B E B H R R

E E E R O S Y

A N M N T R E O

O O L T E C

T T T E I E R A N S

S T B I L A B O

W L Y L E O

Quote: " _ _ _ _ _ _   _ _ _

_ _ _   _ _ _ _ _ ?"

Picture Purr-fect Reflection

To solve this puzzle, start by answering each of the seven clues. The number of spaces indicate the number of letters in the answer words. Then transfer the letters corresponding to the numbers into the quotation spaces to reveal picture purr-fect reflection by poet Robert Southey.

1. Altitude

__ __ __ __ __ __
25 24 23 5 25 6

2. Gaffe

__ __ __ __ __ __ __
16 22 13 8 27 24 18

3. Observed

__ __ __
15 11 30

4. Snake

__ __ __
16 35 11

5. Picture

__ __ __ __ __
23 3 11 5 24

6. Created

__ __ __ __
3 11 27 24

7. Body of water __ __ __ __
           22 11 10 24

Quotation:

__ __ __ __ __ __ __ __ __,
11 10 23 6 6 24 8 23 15

__ __ __ __ __ __ __ __ __ __ __
23 8 6 25 24 11 8 23 3 11 22

__ __ __ __ __, __ __ __ __
30 35 18 22 27 30 25 11 6

__ __ __ __ __ __ __ __
11 18 35 15 24 16 13 27

__ __ __ __ __ __ __
23 15 23 8 6 25 24

__ __ __ __ __ __.
5 11 18 27 24 8

Proverbial Cats

Cats figure into many common proverbs, idioms, and expressions. In each sentence, circle the word that completes the saying.

1. Say something! Or has the cat got your (VOICE, TONGUE, WORDS)?

2. A cat may look at a (KING, MOUSE, TIGER).

3. Cats have nine (LOSSES, LIVES, LOVES).

4. When the cat's away, the (KITTENS, PUPPIES, MICE) will play.

5. Those two fight like cats and (DOGS, WOLVES, RATS).

6. Happy is the (HUG, HOME, HAND) with at least one cat in it.

7. The dog may be wonderful prose, but only the cat is (POETRY, PRAISEWORTHY, MELODIC).

8. All cats love (SOUP, STEW, FISH), but fear their wet paws!

9. Those who'll play with cats must expect to be (HISSED AT, SCRATCHED, BATTED).

10. A cornered cat becomes as fierce as a (DOG, APE, LION).

11. We need one person to take on this dangerous task. So who will volunteer to (BELL, CHASE, CAPTURE) the cat?

12. It was supposed to be a secret! Why did you let the cat out of the (HOUSE, BAG, CAR)?

13. Why is she so self-satisfied? She looks like the cat that ate the (FISH, CANARY, MOUSE).

14. Please! Stop (BOUNCING, JOKING, PUSSYFOOTING) around and tell me the truth!

15. It's (RAINING, SLEETING, ICING) cats and dogs outside.

16. After so long an illness, she's as weak as a (CAT, KITTEN, MOUSE).

Paws to Ponder

There are things to ponder about in this puzzle.

ACROSS

1. "It's sure __ to chase a 5-Down around a little!!"
4. Roman cats' debate venue
6. "That's an ancestor of mine—the big guy."
7. Human's best response to cat's demand
9. Cat of many years
10. French affirmation
11. Afternoon nap time (Abbr.)
12. Corrode, like metal
13. "It's something to lick off my human's dinner plate."
15. "She says this every time I bring her something from outside."

DOWN

1. "Put it in my bowl—now!"
2. Large metal container with a tap
3. "N" in the Greek alphabet
4. "The great ones put cats in starring roles."

DOWN CON'T.

5. House rodent
6. Snip
8. Newborn cat
10. "One little claw scratch,
    and this is what she says!"
12. Convenient cat scratching item
14. Gold (Abbr.)

Journey With A Friend

There are 9 differences between these two pictures – can you find them all?

Cat and Mouse Maze

Help the mouse scamper to the safety of his house in the middle of the maze!

It's a Feline World

Find each bolded word in the word search grid!

Keyboards are for **sleeping**,
Stairways are for naps...
Your cell phone is for adding
Funny **kitten apps**.

TP in the bathroom
Is for feline **kicks**...
All **food** on **kitchen** counters
Gets a few good **licks**.

Curtains hang for **climbing**,
Carpets spread to **shred**...
And any **chair** you sit on,
Off! It's now my **bed**!

Yes, each and every **morning**,
You can clearly see
The grand old sun **arising**
Just to **shine** on me!

```
H F U D J A J M N J R I B U K
W E X F S X W N Z G K X Q E J
S L E E P I N G J W U K Y G L
O I M U X W F D X H A B H F J
D K N U I S O L N G O K L G Z
R K I C K S O C H A J W R K X
Z U Y T A R D L R E K F J A D
N I P I T Z X D Y E S K C I L
M C B W P E S A Y C I R Q T Z
U O D B A G N K V J C H D E B
B M R K B N F A I P H H F E C
U Y J N L S G K P H G H A H G
T C X M I B Y N A P F U A F Y
R M X U L N T A I K S I F T O
D O K T O L G V W S R R K X U
S R N X O U F B A R I M C R E
O L A V K L S L C B I R J O V
G V S T C I U G M R N A A Z J
P N V L K F T Z N G K F T Y Q
Q K M I D O W L B I W D K S I
T I S N E H C T I K B R G B B
Y R R N O A D Q E E F M Y G R
T D I F T S H R E D F T I W B
W H B H V S X S V L F C J L N
S C U R T A I N S N F B V U C
```

Cat Nap

When might these professionals take time out for a cat nap?

Here are your clues.

When:

1. They don't have class:

   _____

2. The daily grind gets them down:

   _____

3. They can't keep their feet on the ground:

   _____

4. They're tired of being punctual:

   _____

5. They're no longer well-grounded:

   _____

6. They're tired of dishing it out:

_____

7. They don't feel noteworthy:

_____

8. They have found all the missing links:

_____

9. They've been to enough board meetings:

_____

10. They realize they have a herd mentality:

_____

11. They're not patient anymore:

_____

12. They feel unloved on court:

_____

Awww!

How cute can you get? This puzzle includes quite a few "cute" words!

ACROSS

1. Ad
6. Before (prefix)
9. East Indian herb
12. Eagle's nest
13. Permissive
14. Support position (Abbr.)
15. Polynesian island
16. Choose
17. Ball holder
18. Tinted
20. Oriental
22. Attractive
25. Countless
26. Bronzed
27. Fermented
29. Freshened
31. Entertaining
32. Flightless birds
36. Artificially reddened
39. Tire meas.
40. New Testament epistle writer
43. Well-__, supporter
45. Explode
46. Invitation abbreviation
47. Conger
48. "Coochie-__!"
50. Tiny amounts
54. Traveler's aid
55. Strange or odd
56. Female relative
57. Where the Prodigal Son worked
58. Pup's cry
59. Excite

DOWN

1. Cave dweller
2. Lion's name
3. Pot
4. "At thy __ hand there are pleasures..." (Psa. 16:11)
5. Loveliness
6. Trudge
7. Music genre

DOWN CON'T

8. Surviving
9. Courtyard
10. Perfect
11. Alter
19. Gorgeous sight
21. Eye problem
22. School org.
23. Jogged
24. Wind dir.
25. Headlines section (2 words)
28. Summer mo. Abvr.
30. Enfold
33. Highway sign subj.
34. Operate
35. Gent's title
37. Uproar
38. God's attribute
40. Appears to be
41. Something for a good dog
42. Orange juice descriptor
44. Go bad
46. Dog's playtime, maybe
49. Paris affirmative
51. Afternoon beverage
52. Take on a role
53. "I was blind, now I __" (John 9:25)

Joyful Kitty

Life has a way of bringing joyful surprises and delightful happenings into our day! Here's a puzzle chockfull of them! One word has been added to get you started.

4 LETTERS
Love
Moon

5 LETTERS
Birth
Bloom
Earth
Gifts
Light
Smile
Songs
Stars

6 LETTERS
Angels
Family
Growth
Guests
Heaven
Melody
Plenty
Praise
Reward
Spirit
Sweets
Treats
Visits

7 LETTERS
Dessert
Flowers
Kittens
Puppies
Sunbeam
Tickles
Wonders

8 Letters
Children
Kindness
Laughter
Optimism
Sparkles

9 LETTERS
Abundance
Butterfly
Chocolate

12 LETTERS
~~Celebrations~~
Thanksgiving

CELEBRATIONS

Furry Friends

Quick! How many words of four letters or more can you form from the word FRIENDSHIP? No letter can be used more times than it appears in the word friendship; no plurals, past tenses, or capitalized words. Common, everyday words only! We found 32!

F R I E N D S H I P

_____ _____ _____ _____

_____ _____ _____ _____

_____ _____ _____ _____

_____ _____ _____ _____

_____ _____ _____ _____

_____ _____ _____ _____

_____ _____ _____ _____

_____ _____ _____ _____

Litter Mates

One year, a prize-winning cat bore
a litter of four littens. Two years later,
her litter was 1½ times that big.
How many kittens were in
the second litter?

A Litter of Kittens

A litter of kittens is all too cute! See how many groups of animals and bunches of things you can correctly name!

1. Finches
   a. Charm
   b. Chain
   c. Chatter

2. Firewood
   a. Cable
   b. String
   c. Cord

3. Owls
   a. Parliament
   b. Senate
   c. Congress

4. Leopards
   a. Leap
   b. Spot
   c. Roar

5. Hay
   a. Baal
   b. Bail
   c. Bale

6. Broccoli
   a. Bunch
   b. Floret
   c. Clove

7. Rabbits
   a. Draw
   b. Fluffle
   c. Sketch

8. Grapes
   a. Bunch
   b. Branch
   c. Bundle

9. Mice
   a. Kin
   b. Trap
   c. Family

10. Books
    a. Bibliophile
    b. Reads
    c. Series

11. Badgers
    a. Town
    b. Colony
    c. Herd

12. Ferrets
    a. Business
    b. Corporation
    c. Department

13. Newspapers
    a. Stand
    b. Bundle
    c. Copy

14. Clams
    a. School
    b. Rout
    c. Bed

15. Rattlesnakes
    a. Samba
    b. Cha cha
    c. Rhumba

16. Cars
    a. Fleet
    b. Parking lot
    c. Drove

17. Cookies
    a. Bake
    b. Batch
    c. Bundle

18. Hinds
    a. Acre
    b. Lot
    c. Parcel

Cuddly Kitties

Answers to clues in this puzzle are pairs of alliterative words, like "cute kittens." The spaces tell you how many letters are in each word.

1. Newlywed woman's parakeets

——————— —————

2. Thespian's pranks

—————— ——————

3. Jovial supper

————— ————

4. Most-favored rye

———— —————

5. Curled potato crisps

—————— —————

6. Antagonist pachyderm

— ————— ——————————

7. Tacky kelp

———————   ———————

8. Quiet domicile

——————   —————

9. Silent butterfly

—————   ———————

10. Irritable reply

——————   ———————

11. Notable banner

——————   —————

12. Resurrection Day festivity

——————   —————

13. Poised daughter

————————   —————

14. Cheap writing instrument

——————   ——————

Mothers Love

In column 1, there's a word commonly associated with mothers. The letters are in order, but they're mixed with unneeded letters. Match the column 1 word with the correct arrangement of white spaces in column 2! The first one is done for you.

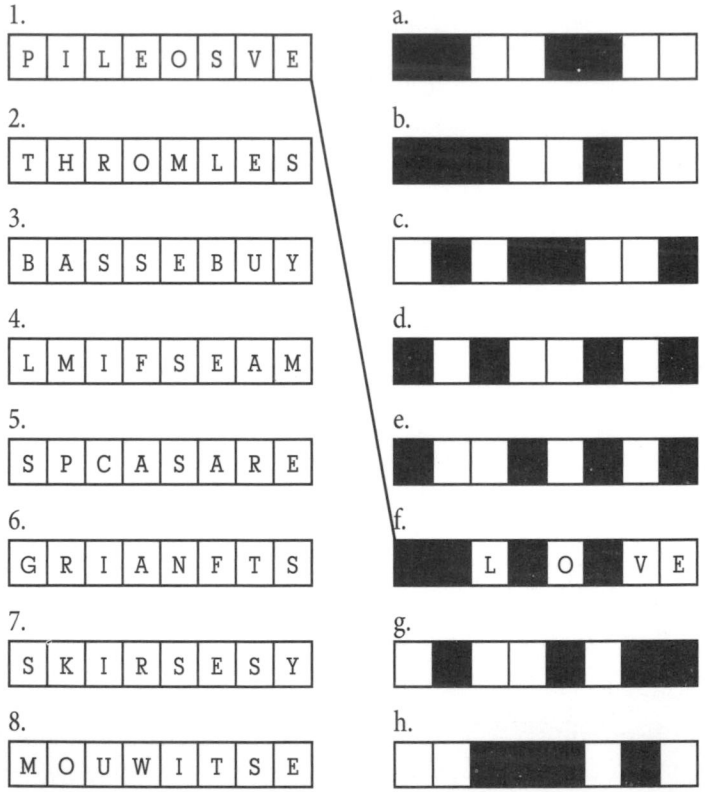

1. P I L E O S V E
2. T H R O M L E S
3. B A S S E B U Y
4. L M I F S E A M
5. S P C A S A R E
6. G R I A N F T S
7. S K I R S E S Y
8. M O U W I T S E

a.
b.
c.
d.
e.
f. L O V E
g.
h.

EEEEEK!!

The answer to each clue is a word with a long "e" sound!

1. Insect: _ _ _ _ _ _

2. Playground equipment: _ _ _ _ _ _ _

3. Sheep's coat: _ _ _ _ _ _ _

4. Explorer: _ _ _ _ _ _ _ _

5. Protection: _ _ _ _ _ _ _

6. African cat: _ _ _ _ _ _ _ _

7. Spring holiday: _ _ _ _ _ _ _

8. Church elder: _ _ _ _ _ _ _

9. Ardor: _ _ _ _

10. Staffer: _ _ _ _ _ _ _ _

I Am A Cat

Find each bolded word in the word search grid!

I am a **CAT**

and I do as I **please**–

Like **ambush** the **mouse**

and **nibble** its **cheese**.

I **worry** the **fish**

whenever I **wish**,

And I **might** take my **nap**

on your dinner **dish**.

Yes, I am a CAT–

And **THAT** is THAT!

```
N N V O E D I I V M B A L L W
E L W T I Z N B G O O C H O A
U L Z S A W N A N P F U Q H N
Z Y H Z D C V D P D K A S V B
O E V I X R Z D G Y F N U E G
E K S P M V R X K K A O T K T
L M E E X Y O X P Q K T A H T
N L O D E T H P B T W A K H Q
Q U Z I H H F F A Y C U C Z H
X W E N T E C M L V N Z Q P O
R D L L Y T M Q D W K O N A V
Q H B E E Y O G I M H E E F S
Z J B H F G O O H E S A E L P
H S I G F C T G D T W X Z A H
H C N X Y O U L W Y U P S P V
U W L M Q L D Y N V F D P J G
B R C E G R W P L G O S Y G H
W R Y K K Z F H N Z D Q C E O
I Y D U Y J T X C I I H S I F
O F Q I C V K B Q O T O H Y L
H Z E V Z W C L G I T S A M C
S U L H T A N L R H U X W Q Z
I K Q W V B M Z G B O P T F N
W T K P U Q J I M O D F J F R
Y W O R R Y M A R G I G R F H
```

Tricky Feline

Complete this puzzle by adding at least one letter on both sides of the letter combination to make a common uncapitalized word. No plurals allowed. Use as few letters as possible!

1. _____ LB _____

2. _____ MF _____

3. _____ XC _____

4. _____ NC _____

5. _____ TC _____

6. _____ NL _____

7. _____ TL _____

8. _____ CN _____

9. _____ TR _____

10. _____ LG _____

11. _____ KR _____

12. _____ BL _____

13. _____ SD _____

14. _____ DW _____

15. _____ GR _____

16. _____ YS _____

17. _____ DV _____

18. _____ NS _____

19. _____ YM _____

Feline Happiness

Every day, there are so many things that make life wonderful. See if you can find the ones in this puzzle!

Kittens	Laughter
Flowers	Prayer
Puppies	Enthusiasm
Canaries	Happiness
Music	Giving
Songs	Children
Love	Babies
Family	Birth
Friends	Renewal
Sunny skies	Recreation
Mountains	Relaxation
Sunsets	Fulfillment
Kindness	Satisfaction
Joy	Glad heart

```
S Y C T G S U N S E T S E C E
C X R L Y J Y S B E S G N O S
B U A H O E X I D Y E O K V D
G K P Y K N R J Q N X W H X R
L E G S X T E T B G E T C E X
A U N E H H M R O A K I C P M
D E I I F U L C D H B R R O A
H W V K L S W S D L E I U F G
E F I S N I H P E A I N E F L
A X G Y L A C N T I T H U S F
R H Y N A S A I Z A R L C G H
T T U N U M O R I Y F A X K P
S Z L U G N J N Q I S B N K S
A C A S H G S C L E O V I A Q
T A W D T C N L I S L N T B C
R C E X E U M P N J D I U N R
U I N G R E P E U N S B O P L
H S E O N U T B E F O I D C K
J U R T P T Q S A H T K A R M
H M D N I J S C X A S R U I K
Z A I K A E T S X N D E V O L
F K N N I I M A R E Y A R P M
B B X N O G L K S R E W O L F
I R H N X E F A M I L Y O R G
S Q F O R X S S E N I P P A H
```

Solutions

Page 6: 1. Sleep, 2. Playful, 3. Loving, 4. Groomer
5. Rub, 6. Breed, 7. Domestic, 8. Catnip, 9. Patches

Page 7:

Eat	Lot	Pal	Pry	Say	Sty
Ail	Eon	Nap	Par	Ran	Set	Tap
Ale	Lap	Nay	Pay	Rap	Sip	Tar
Ant	Lay	Net	Pen	Ray	Sir	Tie
Any	Let	Nit	Per	Rip	Sly	Ton
Ape	Lie	Not	Pet	Rot	Son	Yap
Apt	Lip	Oat	Pie	Rye	Sot	Yet
Are	Lit	One	Pot	Sat	Soy	Yip

Page 8:

Page 9: Hiss, Tiger, Jump, Nap, Attitude, Fish, Scent
MITTENS

Page 10/11:

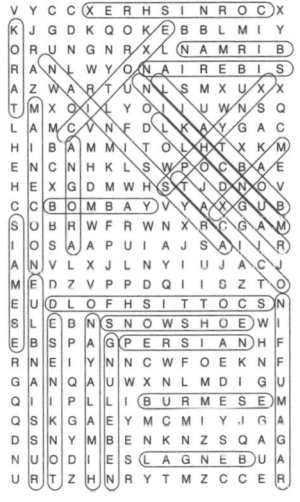

Page 15:

Page 12/13:

Fur, For; Kibble, Nibble; Cute, Mute; Purr, Purl; Tabby, Gabby; Claws, Claps; Play, Pray; Scent, Scene; Patches, Matches; Hiss, Hips; Six, Nix

Page 14: The second offer would bring in $5,120 at the end of 12 months.

Page 16:

Page 17:

Jones: Seed packet,
Brown: Sunglasses,
Smith: Towel,
Dorel: Moitten,
Hansen: Sun visor

Page 18/19:

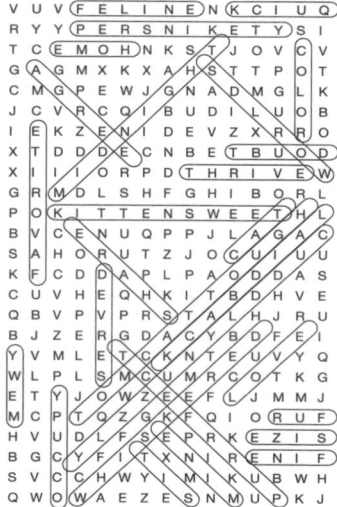

Page 20:

1. Catfish
2. Windowsill
3. Flowerbed
4. Armchair
5. Sunbeam
6. Troublemaker
7. Catnap
8. Copycat
9. Fishbowl
10. Plaything
11. Showoff
12. Sweetheart

Page 21: If the puppy takes two bones, the game's over!

Page 22: Callie is telling the truth; all the other statements agree, and there is only one statement of the five that is true.

Page 23: ROSTER, SPROUT, BLOSSOM, TOURIST
Caption: SOURPUSS

Page 24/25: If a dog jumps into your lap, it is because he is fond of you; but if a cat does the same thing, it is because your lap is warmer.
Alfred North Whitehead

Page 26: 1. Leopard, 2. Bobcat, 3. Lion, 4. Jaguar
5. Puma 6. Cougar, 7. Tiger

Page 27: 1. Clowder, 2. Kindle, 3. Streak, 4. Pride
5. Shadow, 6. Leap, 7. Coalition

Page 28/29:

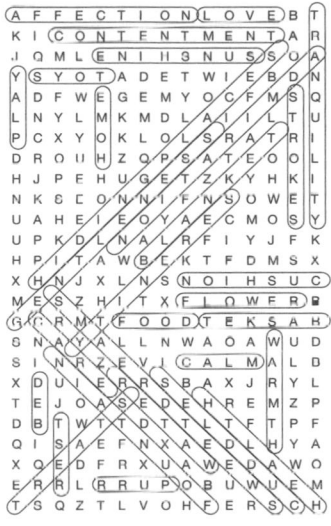

Page 30/31:

1. Nepal, Pallid
2. Play, Layers
3. Sudden, Dental
4. Kabob, Bobtail
5. Pawpaw, Pawned
6. Ocelot, Lotion
7. Supper, Persian
8. Rubbed, Bedrock
9. Appear, Early
10. Indoor, Doorway
11. Rampant, Panther
12. Content, Tentative

Page 32: 2 cans(each)=4 cans

Page 33: Cats are a MYSTERIOUS kind of folk.

Page 34/35: 1. Fish dish, 2. Paw claw, 3. Her fur, 4.
Mew pew, 5. Hissy missy, 6. Litter sitter, 7. Flabby
tabby, 8. Patch match, 9. Pale male, 10. Prowl growl
11. Sole bowl, 12. Mint hint

Page 36/37:
Cat traits

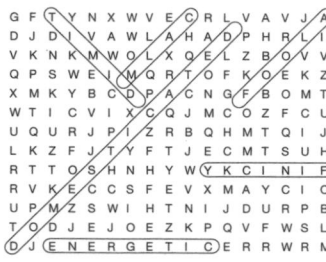

Antonyms

Page 38: 1. MATE, 2. TATERS, 3. SLAVER, 4. PALE
5. SPAN, 6. NARY

Page 39:

Cat	Dog	Cat
Dog	Cat	Dog
Cat	Cat	Cat
Dog	Cat	Dog
Cat	Dog	Cat

Page 40: Armor,
Mouse, Guest,
Starry, Palate
GLAMOUR PUSS

Page 41:
1. LEAP,
2. AWARD,
3. OVUM,
4. PRAISE,
5. VOICE,
6. RETINA,
7. EVE,
8. DIMMER

Page 42:

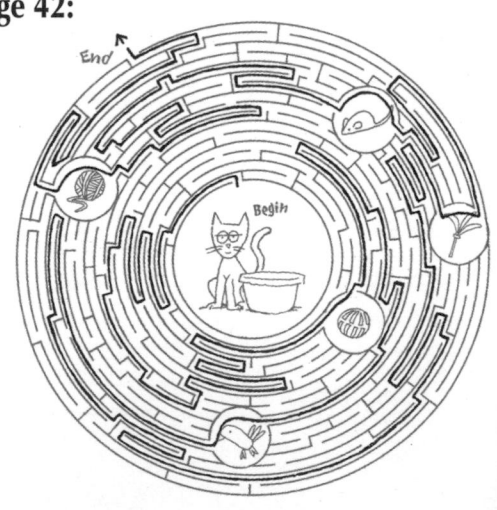

Page 43:

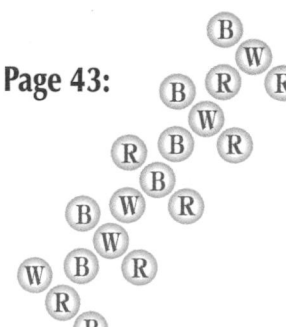

Page 46/47:

1. POLE
2. BALL
3. MOON
4. NAP
5. DOOR
6. EAR
7. BIRTH
8. DOG
9. BIRD
10. ARM
11. PAD
12. HAIR
13. FOOT
14. GOLD
15. PLAY
16. DISH
17. CASE
18. SOFT
19. EYE
20. TOE

Page 44/45:

	C	A	T	S	C	R	A	D	L	E	
1.	C	T	A	S	C	R	A	D	L	E	
2.	C	T	A	S	C	R	A	D	E	L	E
3.	C	T	A	S	C	R	T	D	E	L	E
4.	C	T	R	S	C	A	T	D	E	L	E
5.	C	T	R	S	C	A	T	D	E	L	R
6.	C	T	R	S	C	A	T	D	E	O	R
7.	C	T	R	I	C	A	T	D	E	O	R
8.	C	T	R	I	C	G	T	D	E	O	R
9.	C	T	R	I	N	G	T	D	E	O	R
10.	C	T	R	I	N	G	T	D	E	O	R	Y
11.	S	T	R	I	N	G	T	D	E	O	R	Y
12.	S	T	R	I	N	G	T	H	E	O	R	Y

Page 48:

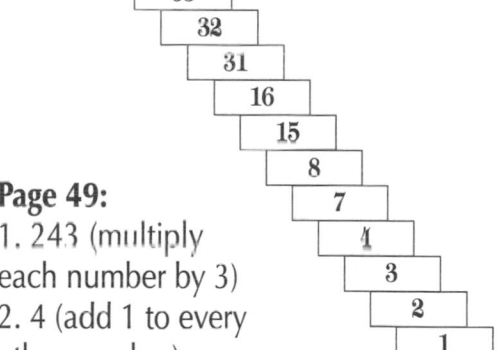

Page 49:

1. 243 (multiply each number by 3)
2. 4 (add 1 to every other number)
3. 256 (multiply each number by itself)
4. 8 (add 1; subtract 2)
5. 12 (divide number in half; add 4)
6. 71 (subtract each number by 6)

Page 50:

				¹AT				²AR
		³AD	OP	TI	ON			OM
		VI		TU		⁴TO	MC	AT
	⁵MI	CE		⁶DE	SE	RT		IC
	DD					OI		
⁷PO	LE	⁸CA	TS		⁹EA	SE	ME	NT
		LI				SH		
		¹⁰CO	ME			EL		
						LS		

Page 54/55:

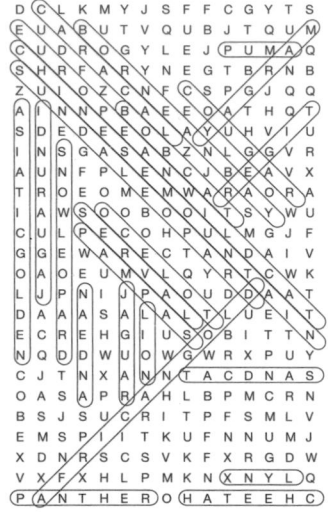

Page 58/59:
1. b, 2. a, 3. a, c
4. c, 5. a, b, c
6. a, 7. b, 8. b

Page 51/52/53:
1. Redder, 2. Peep
3. Top spot, 4. Sis
5. Now I won!
6. Go, dog!
7. Ma has a ham
8. Tuna nut, 9. Pop
10. Was it a cat I
saw?, 11. Taco cat,
12. Rub bur

Page 56/57:
Your answers may vary.
1. FOOT, soot, slot, slat,
slaw, CLAW
2. PURR, pure, lure, lurk,
luck, LICK
3. CURL, cure, core, code,
coda, soda, SOFA
4. PLAY, plat, peat, pest
rest, rapt, raps, NAPS
5. FOOD, fold, hold, hole
hose, hase, hash, dash, DISH
6. COAT, chat, chit, chin,
shin, SKIN
7. HEAD, heal, teal, tell
tall, TAIL
8. NOSE, lose, lore, core,
care, cars, EARS

Page 60/61: Adopt, Anoint, Arena, Dash, Dime, Dome, Hint, Hoed, Hoer, Hone, Honed, Item, Mane, Meat, Memoir, Mime, Moan, Mode, Name, Neon, Node, Nosh, Odeon, Opinion, Option, Pane, Pate, Pint, Point, Rash, Ride, Rite, Shin, Ship, Shod, Shone, Shop, Tide, Time, Trim, Trio

Page 62/63: 1. Stretch, 2. Chase, 3. Serene, 4. Nestle, 5. Least, 6. Stroke, 7. Kennel, 8. Elusive, 9. Vest, 10. Stripe, 11. Pedigree, 12. Eerie

Page 64/65/66:
Cat Naps: Chair, Patio, Cushion, Bin, Shelf, Closet
Cat Treats: Tuna, Chicken, Beef, Gravy, Salmon, cheese
Cat Kinds: Siamese, Persian, Ragdoll, Maine Coon, Russian Blue, **Cat Toys:** Foil Ball, Feather, Plush mouse, Sunbeam, Rolling Bell, **Saying:** Any time is a purrfect time to spend in the company a cat!

Page 67: Callie: Chicken in gravy, Lady Gray: Meaty Pâté, Ebony: Fish Pâté, Tom: Beef in gravy, Snowball: Flaked salmon

Page 68/69:

```
A B M E D E R A P S G Y X B D X D
G T P E Q G V F F G F R S V E K O
G L I L F Z D U A G P E I W A D Z
A I J M E W B A I P B M Z T R S O
O B F W E A E V T Z E A K B Y T V
L E F Q W O S K V I A I T S U N Y
L S T W L L J E R P S N D S M T A
P T I Z Z O E R Q C T B Y O A A D
H V V G W E V Y X B S U S D H E B
G S X E R U S E L O T T L M E L L
O X M P I T E L L W E X Q J A C T
R T M P V O Z C Q X L I H R U B
E Z U A N N A G W D O T J U S T J
H V T J Y C N N Z V H S Y C O U K
N Y V T O Y Q A Y F H E X Y D S O E
U F M U T P J E Z O S A U A W T S
E Z X N U N L F C I S L C Y W O U
V S J Y E I B L A X U M T B H A R
O P F V M N P R Z O D E T R E L A
L O L G Y L P Y G S G C A R E W N
```

Page 68/69 Cont'd:

I've been **alerted** –
at **least** so I **hear**
that your home could **use** a cat –
Not just any old critter,
But the **best** of all **beasts**,
A **dear** and **lovely** cat!

Sure, I'll need a few things
Like water and food –
Plus **any** treats you can **spare**,
But mostly I desire
Your **praise**, **love**, and **care** (acre).

An **angel** ? **Most** of the **time**!
My **ways** can be **rowdy**,
Yet I'll bring a **smile** and happiness
to your heart.
So, **may** I come in?
Say "yes," if you **please**
And you'll **remain** a **hero**
to me forever!

Page 70/71:
1. Va**ca**tion
2. Cari**ca**ture
3. Edu**ca**tion
4. S**cat**hing
5. Mus**cat**
6. Advo**ca**te
7. S**cat**tered
8. Lo**ca**te
9. Equivo**ca**te
10. Toc**ca**ta
11. Abdi**ca**te
12. Communi**cat**e

Page 72/73:

180

Page 74/75: Looks like you have some money in the kitty!

Page 76/77: 1. HUNT, 2. CLAW, 3. LEAP, 4. TAIL 5. TICK, 6. DIET

Page 78: 1. b, 2. c, 3. c, 4. a, 5. b

Page 79: 1) Lamp base moved 2) Cat on chair, tail repositioned, 3) Chair arm wing is smaller 4) Birds moved 5) Cat in window smaller, 6) Picture smaller 7) Outlet moved 8) Stripped cat moved 9) Drapes shortened

Page 80/81: 1. Team/Meat, 2. Peek/Keep, 3. Foal/Loaf 4. Teas/Seat, 5. What/Thaw, 6. Tarp/Part, 7. Pear/Reap 8. Lilt/Till, 9. Tool/Loot, 10. Host/Tosh

Page 82/83: Patches, as only one of the kittens was telling the truth. Biscuit, as only one of the cats was telling the truth.

Page 84: WHISKERS: **K**eepsake, Ic**I**cle, Lengt**H**, Coa**S**ter, Ar**R**ival, Th**W**art, Se**c**r**E**t, Le**S**son HOUSECAT: Scat**T**er, Am**A**teur, M**U**sic, Inc**H**ing, Ta**S**ty, **C**oddle, Spo**O**ky, L**E**ader

Page 85: Step 1: Place one kitten in each pan. You might find the lighter kitten immediately. Step 2: If the two are equal weight, place another kitten in each pan. The pan that goes up reveals the lightest kitten.

Page 86/87:

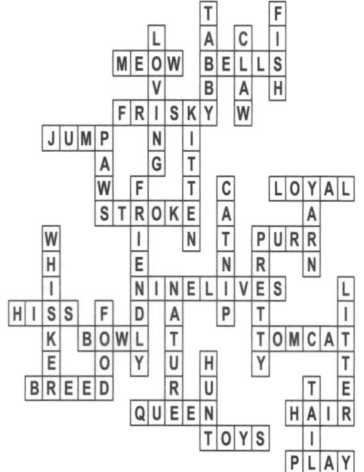

Page 88/89:

Page 90: A cat is a lion in a jungle of small bushes.

Page 91: 1. Reptile, 2. Clowder, glaring, 3. Hand 4. Flavor, food, 5. Church, 6. Happiness, joy

Page 92: A cat, I am sure, could walk on a cloud without coming through.

Page 93: 1. He thought, the cut was caused by a f**ang or a** claw. 2. "Send a **wire! Hair**-raising things are happening!" he shouted. 3. "Pick up the **tab," by**standers laughed. 4. "The cat's in that tree?" she asked. "Jee**pers!" I an**swered. 5. Oh, **man, x**-rays cinched the diagnosis. 6. She went out looking like a **ragamuffin**. 7. In the **snow, shoe**s are mandatory.

Page 94/95:

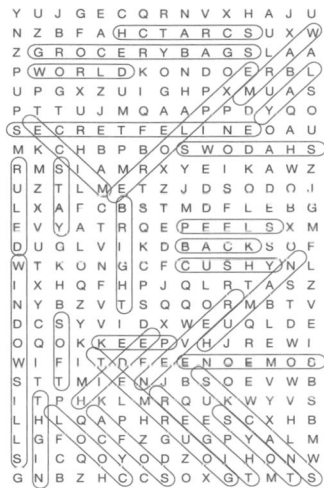

Page 96: 67 ½ feet

Page 98/99:

Page 100: Marmalade

Page 97: 1. It is a palindrome - the phrase can be read forward or backward. 2. Each word is an example of onomatopoeia – it is reflects the sound associated with it. 3. The phrase is alliterative – each word begins with the same sound. 4. Each pair is an anagram – just re-arrange the letters! 5. Each word is spelled consonant/vowel/consonant repeated.

Page 101: Fill the 8 oz. container with water and pour it into the 10 oz. container. Fill the 8 oz. container again, but this time pour the water into the 7 oz. container. Add the remaining 1 oz. to the 10 oz. container for a total of 9 oz.

Page 102:
1. Sofa, Ball, Leaf,
2. Food, Toys, Desk
3. Tree, Bird, Sand

Page 103:
One – only the
narrator was going
to St. Ives!

Page 106:
All the names are
also common nouns.

Page 107:
Persian, Burmese, Himalayan, Bengal, Russian Blue,
Siamese, Abyssinian, Ragdoll, Birman, Maine Coon

Page 104/105:

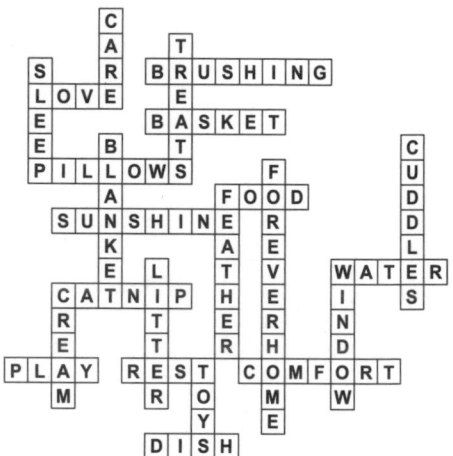

Page 108:

9	5	1
4	3	8
2	7	6

Page 109:

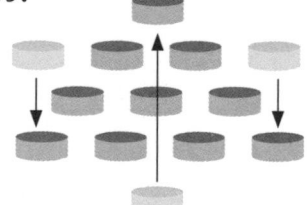

Page 110:

SCR	AM	BLE		MOU
	IA		PO	SER
A	BLE		ET	
CED		FUR	RY	
	FIN	NISH		SUN
OR	DER	ED		SHI
ATE			NI	NE

Page 111:
Judy: Gray Tom, Marilyn: Orange Tom, Jerry: Gray Female & Black Female, Lois: White Female

Page 112/113:
1. Scarce, Common, 2. Unite, Divide, 3. Float, Sink
4. Raise, Lower, 5. Fresh, Stale, 6. Praise, Blame
7. Expand, Contract, 8. Close, Distant, 9. Rapid, Sluggish
10. Inner, Outer, 11. Rude, Polite, 12. Lenient, Strict

Page 114:
1. Spaniel, a breed of dog; the rest are cat breeds.
2. Milk, a liquid; the rest are styles of canned cat food.
3. Parsley, an herb of the Apiaceae or Umbelliferae family; the others are varieties of mint (Lamiaceae family). 4. Veterinarian, a physician for animals; the rest are dietary choices.

Page 115:
Note that *all three envelopes* are labeled incorrectly! All Amanda needs to do is open the envelope labeled First Prize. If a $35 gift card is in it, it is Second Prize; if a $25 gift card is in it, it is Third Prize. Since she knows that the other two envelopes are mislabeled, she can simply switch the labels.

Page 116/117:
1. a, 2. a, 3. c, 4. a, 5. b, 6. c, 7. b, 8. a, 9. c, 10. a

Page 118/119:

Page 120/121:

Page 125:

```
FRURYLABLFR
URYLABLFRUR
YLABLFRURYL
ABLFRURYLAB
LFRURYLABLF
RURYLABLLRU
RYLABLFAURY
LABLFRBRYLA
BLFRUYYLABL
FRURRLABLFR
URYRABLFRUR
YLUBLFRURYL
FFURYLABLFR
UFYLABLFRUR
YLABLFRURYL
ABLFRURYLAB
LFRURYLABLF
RURYLABLFRU
RYLABLFRURY
LABLFRURYLA
BLFRURYLABL
FRURYLABLFR
```

Page 122/123:
1. Please, 2. Chowder, 3. Quest,
4. Moat, 5. Glean, 6. Slaw,
7. Lowly, 8. Trip, 9. Groan,
10. Skate

Page 124:

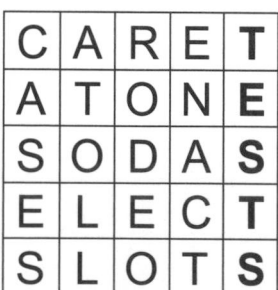

Page 126/127
Quotation: A cat pours his body on the floor like water.

Page 128/129:

Page 130
God made the cat to give man the pleasure of stroking a tiger.

Page 131
Four – each sister kitten had the same brother kitten

Page 134
1. Rouse, 2. Parole, 3. Sprain, 4. Raves, 5. Loams

Page 135
Typist, Copilot, Private, Accent, Answer: Because they're COPYCATS!

Page 132/133:

Page 136

C	A	T	N	I	P
P	O	U	N	C	E
C	A	L	I	C	O
T	O	M	C	A	T
S	T	R	I	P	E
T	R	E	A	T	S
F	R	I	S	K	Y

Page 137:
1. Nap, 2. Call, 3. Up, 4. Walk, 5. Word, 6. Tail

Page 138/139:

Cat & Holly	Angel Cat	Angel Cat	Cat Orna-ment	Cat & Tree
Large	Small	Small	Large	Small
Large	Large	Cat Plaque	Large	Large
Small	Large	Large	Large	Small
Fabric	Yarn	Straw	Yarn	Fabric

Page 140:

1.

P	A	T	H
A	C	H	E
W	R	E	N
S	E	E	S

2.

D	A	M	P
A	L	E	E
M	O	O	T
S	E	W	S

3.

A	L	I	T
M	O	D	E
E	V	E	S
N	E	A	T

Page 141:
1. Catamaran
2. Shrubbery
3. Eyesore
4. Ornament
5. Ocelot
6. Interstate
7. Bobtails
8. Yellow
Quote: Tabby or not tabby?

Page 142/143:
1. Height, 2. Blunder, 3. Saw, 4. Boa, 5. Image, 6. Made, 7. Lake
Quote: A kitten is, in the animal world, what a rosebud is in the garden.

Page 144/145:
1. Tongue, 2. King, 3. Lives, 4. Mice, 5. Dogs, 6. Home, 7. Poetry, 8. Fish, 9. Scratched, 10. Lion, 11. Bell, 12. Bag, 13. Canary, 14. Pussyfooting, 15. Raining, 16. Kitten

Page 146/147:

	F	U	N		
F	O	R	U	M	
L	I	O	N		O	K
O	L	D		O	U	I
P	M		R	U	S	T
	S	A	U	C	E	
		U	G	H		

Page 149:

Page 148:

Differences Solution: 1) Blade of grass added on sidewalk 2) Tree trunk on left longer 3) Pine tree on left moved 4) Hill added in background 5) Striped cat front paw moved 6) Kitty moved forward 7) Blade of grass removed in front of house 8) Window bigger 9) Bird added on top of house

Page 150/151:

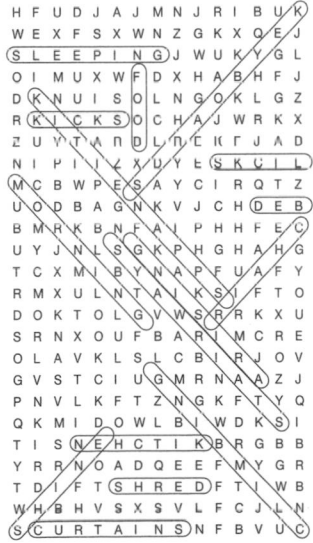

Page 152/153:

Possible Answers:
1. Teachers, professors, instructors, educators
2. Optometrists, lens makers, Barista
3. Astronauts, Pilots
4. Proofreaders, copy editors
5. Electricians
6. Cooks, servers, chefs
7. Musicians
8. Webmasters
9. Carpenters, builders
10. Ranchers, dairy farmers
11. Doctors, physicians
12. Tennis players

Page 154/155:

Page 156/157:

Page 158:
Dine, Diner, Dire, Dish, Drip, Fend, Fiend, Find, Fine, Fire, Fish, Fried, Herd, Hind, Hire, Pend, Pied, Pier, Pine, Pride, Rend, Ride, Rife, Rind, Ripe, Send, Shin, Shine, Ship, Shire, Spend, Spire

Page 159:
Six

Page 160/161:
1. a, 2. c, 3. a, 4. a, 5. c, 6. a, 7. b, 8. a, 9. c, 10. c, 11. b
12. a, 13. b, 14. c, 15. c, 16. a, 17. b, 18. c

Page 162/163:
1. Bride's birds, 2. Actor's antics, 3. Merry meal
4. Best bread, 5. Frizzy fries, 6. Enemy elephant
7. Sticky seaweed, 8. Hushed home, 9. Mute monarch
10. Angry answer, 11. Famous flag, 12. Easter event
13. Graceful girl, 14. Penny pencil

Page 164:	**Page 165:**	**Page 166/167:**
1. F, love	1. Beetle	
2. D, home	2. Seesaw	
3. H, baby	3. Fleece	
4. G, life	4. Pioneer	
5. A, care	5. Shield	
6. C, gift	6. Cheetah	
7. E, kiss	7. Easter	
8. B, wise	8. Deacon	
	9. Zeal	
	10. Employee	

Page 168/169:

Possible answers:
1. Elbow,
2. Comfort,
3. Excuse,
4. Inch,
5. Etch,
6. Inlet,
7. Title,
8. Picnic,
9. Citrus,
10. Algae,
11. Okra,
12. Able,
13. Wisdom,
14. Indwell,
15. Ogre,
16. Mystery,
17. Advice,
18. Sense
19. Payment

Page 170/171:

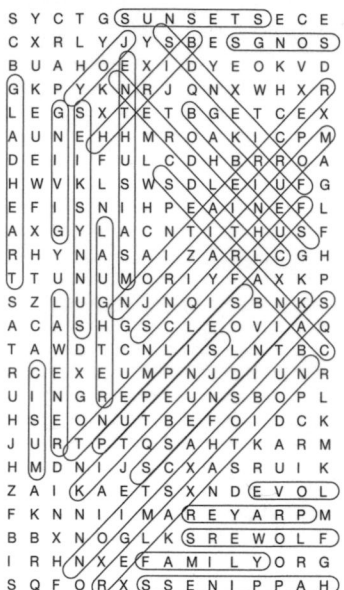

Happy is the home with at least one cat.
Proverb